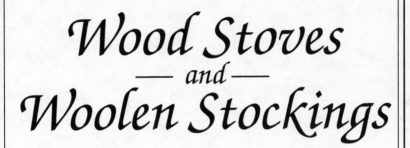

# Wood Stoves
## — and —
# Woolen Stockings

**A vivid and delightful
portrayal of Mormon life
in the early 1900's.**

# Ann Godfrey Hansen

**Covenant**

Communications, Inc.

Covenant Communications, Inc.
Printed in the United States of America
Library of Congress Catalog Card Number 90-084958
Wood Stoves and Woolen Stockings
Printed January 1991
ISBN 1-55503-303-2

*To my parents,*

Thomas H. Godfrey, Jr.,
and Ellen Barson Godfrey,
who were born, lived, and died
in Clarkston, Utah

# Acknowledgments

I am sincerely grateful for the help of my teachers at Utah State University. I thank Professor Moyle Q. Rice, Dr. Austin E. Fife, and Mrs. Venita Nielson for their inspiration and suggestions. I also thank my committee members, Dr. Caseel D. Burke, Professor Ira N. Hayward, and Professor Evelyn Wiggins, for their time and practical assistance.

I am indebted for source material and personal recollections to Vilate Dahle, Mattie Goodey, Catherine H. Griffiths, Andrew L. Heggie, Annie H. Jardine, Mary J. Jones, William J. Loosle, Lucy Mickelson, Bessie Rasmussen, Emma Shepherd, William Shepherd, John J. Shumway, and Annie J. Thompson.

# From Ann's Photo Album

The poet has said, "How dear to my heart are the scenes of my childhood."

Ann Godfrey Hansen
Graduation from B.Y. College
in Logan 1919

Ann Godfrey
Hansen
Born 1900

Ann, age 3, and
Brother Seth

Ann, age 8, and
Cousin Mary Godfrey

# From Ann's Photo Album

Ann, working as a school teacher in Dayton, Idaho

"I have tried to portray life as I remember it without adornment— just the simple, peaceful living of a people I shall always love."

Ann Godfrey Hansen

Ann, preparing for church by picking flowers for the podium.

Ann Hansen, age 90, still bright and active, now lives in Brigham City, Utah. Of Clarkston she says, "Only the stillness, the friendliness, and the atmosphere of peace remain and these we must hold and cherish forever."

# Contents

# Introduction

Isolated. I was in the eighth grade when I first remember hearing this word. My little town of Clarkston, Utah, was having a big homecoming party for all former residents, and each one who spoke on the program seemed to like that word in describing our town.

The sound appealed to me. It made me think of fluffy blue snowflakes, huge cakes of dazzling ice, icicles hanging like elongated cornucopias along the eaves of the house, and the white mounds of frosting on Grandma's Christmas fruit cake. The word was pretty to me and so was our town. Green in summer as the Garden of Eden and a vast expanse of white in winter—clear and cold as the north pole.

A few days later, my teacher, Frank Shumway, asked us to write a composition describing our town. I think mine went something like this: "Clarkston is a small town nestling on a side hill. Some people say we have one short leg, but that isn't so. On the west are lofty mountains of majestic grandeur. [I thought that was a fine sentence.] And to the east, north, and south are huge fields of golden grain. When the quaking aspen on the hills turn yellow and the stubble still keeps its cast of gold, a stranger might think he had suddenly come upon one of the golden cities of Cibola. People say we are isolated, and yet we are called the granary of Cache Valley."

Mr. Shumway read my composition with a lot of dignity and said that it was good, then asked, "Where did you get the word *isolated,* at the homecoming?"

1

"Yes sir," I replied turning red.

"We should use new words," he commended. From then on, the word *isolated* was forever mine.

Sometimes I resented the slurs of visitors—that we were out in the sticks or behind the times, that no one had the gumption to get out. They said we had intermarried until we were all short on mental marbles.

We were proud of our town. After all, we had snow in the hills to make ice cream with until late in the summer. What other town could say the same? More than that, we had everything we needed. Our pioneers had built a schoolhouse and a meeting house of native rock. In our schoolhouse we could learn to read and write, which was then considered sufficient as an education; and we could worship God or enjoy recreation in our little chapel.

The father of the ward was the bishop who was both lawgiver and interpreter of the will of the Lord. His word was supreme. He frowned upon undertakers and doctors, and so everybody did. Both interfered with the natural processes of God and were an uncalled-for expense and luxury.

We were self-sufficient. We could take care of the sick ourselves. The store stocked castor oil, senna leaves, epsom salts, asafetida, and vermifuge for worms in children, and that took care of most of our medical needs.

Three women helped deliver the babies; Aunt Caroline, tall and stern and commanding, Aunt Martha, a prim little Englishwoman with her hair in a little bob on top of her head, and Aunt Agnes, always immaculate in a fresh white apron with knitted lace along the bottom. Birth was a natural process that worried no one; and if complications ever set in, we children did not know about it. These women were on call night and day for the sum of eight dollars—less if you couldn't afford that.

Uncle Jack, with his long curled, white mustache, set the broken bones and always told jokes during the painful process. Uncle Jim, the painstaking carpenter, made the caskets of native lumber and lined them with white outing flannel. Sometimes he covered them with black or white velvet depending on what was available, but the dead never wanted for a neat, substantial coffin. Short and stocky Uncle Joe led the choir and fiddled for the dances.

Our town was laid out in blocks, three north and south and three east and west, with houses on both sides of the road. The architecture of the homes was very similar. People built first a two-room house; then as their family and finances increased, they added a kitchen and dining room and connected them with a large L-shaped porch. Every back yard had a well with a bucket tied to a rope and fastened to the curb. There was a chopping block sprinkled with chicken blood; among the chips lay rooster heads with glazed, half-open eyes, mute evidence of many a fine dinner. In the corner stood a whitewashed privy stocked with a can of ashes and a Sears Roebuck catalog, and sometimes some old newspapers. Here one could retire with impunity and rest or read. Every lot had a row of plum trees. Under them sat a few farm implements profusely sprinkled with droppings of chickens and birds. Close by, the straw-covered stable sheltered a team and a scrub cow or two. Nearby stood a log hen house without windows. Five or six sleek porkers peeked up over a crude pen, and these, with the dog, a few cats, and the roosters, completed each barnyard orchestra.

There was no need for locks or bars on the doors in our little town. Neighbors shared freely. Starts of yeast went from house to house, along with bread and fresh honey, followed at butchering time, with choice meat. We all knew the teaching of the good book—"Inasmuch as ye have done it unto the least of these, ye have done it unto me"—and what's more, we followed it. I remember Clarkston as a place of peace, tranquillity, and harmony.

To ourselves, we were not impoverished shut-ins but a fortunate few—people free from the sins of the outside world. In fact, we felt lucky to be born, to live, and to die right in Clarkston. This poem explains how I felt about my home in Clarkston.

## *Home*

Home is a place of love
Of joy, and faith, and prayer
Where I may go with all my woes
For help from those who care.
Home sweet home, the place I love
The shrine that I hold dear.
My feet may leave, but not my heart
The home that I revere.
Home is a bit of heaven
Where memories live and glow,
Where strong arms reach to soothe and cheer
Wherever I may go.

*Ann G. Hansen*

# Section I

# Spring

*The green of spring was emeralds to me.*

# Spring

When spring came and sap was up in the trees, Dad made each of us a whistle. We chose the size of the willow and the length we wanted our whistle to be. Then with his sharp knife that could cut a slice of bologna or remove a sliver, he cut around the middle of the willow and began tapping to loosen the bark. Slowly, he eased the sleeve off, exposing the fresh, tender wood. Next he carved a groove in the wood and slanted the mouthpiece an inch from the top to the back.

"Now blow this way," he would say. "Not too hard, just gently."

And then the chorus began. High notes, shrill notes, soft notes, and a weak peep from the baby. What a chorus! With that quiet twinkle in his eyes that told us he was having fun, too, our dad would stand and survey us.

## Glamour from the outside world

The traveling theater troupe was coming to town. An agent arrived with handbills a few days in advance of the shows and gave two lively boys free tickets to post them on the schoolhouse, on the store and post office, and on the hitching posts in front of the meeting house.

We all showed up, dazzled by real people with fancy names whom we had never seen before. One year, the leading lady's name was Corinne Lavant, a pretty name for a pretty lady. Mother, comfortably a-bulge, said, "There's a name for our new baby!" And so our little sister became Corinne.

The players gave three shows. The first night was a tragedy with a villain and shooting. The next night was a comedy. On the third night, a city slicker wronged an innocent country girl. That was supposed to teach our girls to stay home and marry boys they knew. Sometimes the actors found out names of local people and told jokes or made up songs about them. These never failed to bring down the house. One of the songs was about my Uncle Joe. It ran:

> Three men went a-hunting
> And nothing could they find;
> At last they came to a jackass
> And that they left behind.
> The Englishman said, "Jackass,"
> And the Scotchman, he said, "Nay."
> But the Irishman said, "It's Joe Godfrey,
> I can tell him by his bray."

Uncle Joe had a loud, hearty laugh, but he just looked down at the sleeping child on his lap and wouldn't laugh. Many ribbed him after, but it still wasn't funny to him.

Mother and Dad took us to see all three plays. We took a two-quart bottle of water and a slice of bread for the baby and went early to get a seat by the big stove. I liked to be up close where I could see the big trunks of clothing standing in the wings. Dresses of shiny, soiled satin with lace, low necks, and short sleeves amazed me. I wondered how they could afford all this finery, for these were the days when more than one Sunday dress was considered extravagant. The rouged cheeks, painted lips, and eyebrows were considered a mark of the underworld. It was years before the girls of our town began to paint their eyebrows with a burned match end and the stores stocked a fragrant, liquid base that we used as powder. And it was years longer before any girl dared use lipstick.

# Going to Logan

Going to Logan was the highlight of my young life. Twice yearly, we made the three-hour trip. In the spring, we went to buy summer clothes. I usually got a flower to trim last year's hat and voile for a new dress. I always coaxed for white shoes, but Dad said they were for city folks with paved walks, not for country people where cows and kids shared the same sidewalk. It took several years to persuade him. In the fall, we bought black-but-toned shoes and long-handled underwear for all, and a suit for the boy whose arms dangled the longest from last year's coat. Dad paid the taxes, and the dentist extracted any teeth he thought might ache before spring.

We were all excited for two days before each trip. When Mother called us at 5 a.m., it didn't take us long to jump out of bed and dress in our Sunday best. We climbed into the buggy and wrapped the tan-fringed lap robes about our knees. We were ready.

Our team had mixed feelings. Deck, a bald-faced bay gelding, had his head up and tail in the air, always ready to go. Silv, a bony sorrel mare, was ever willing to let her companion pull the load and her, too. The minute Dad lifted the lines, Deck gave a lunge, and we were off. Dad pulled back on the lines and called him a damned, high-lifed old fool. We grinned at each other, but cautiously, for Dad never cared to be laughed at.

None of us had much appetite that early in the morn-ing, but as we neared Newton, after the first hour of travel, Mother would bring out a sack of sandwiches and raisin-filled cookies that tasted mighty good. There was always a two-quart bottle of water carefully tucked away for the smaller kids who wanted to drink when they could think of nothing else to do. We called Newton "Danish-town" because so many converts from Denmark had settled there. They liked to speak in their native tongue, and I always felt a little odd about them, wondering just whom and what they were talking about. Little did I dream that a Dane just waking up for the morning chores would be my future husband.

During the next hour, we chatted. Dad would tell us who lived on this farm and that one. We wondered how one man could know so many people and live in Clarkston. We crossed the railroad track and passed through a ghost-like town called Alto. The soil was full of alkali, and the crops always looked sickly and yellow. There were a few brown, weather-beaten houses and straw-covered sheds. A small girl looked out from a sagging screen door, and I thought how lonesome she must be. The family washing sprawled over the front fence of one home, and Mother, who always noticed a washing, clucked disapprovingly, "Look at the color of those clothes." Little heads peeked out of windows, and men and women in outside corrals stopped milking and looked us over thoroughly as we waved and jogged along.

As we neared Bear River, I had to choke back horror. The bridge had collapsed a few years previously while some people from Clarkston were on it. Charles Buttars swam after a baby floating downstream and saved it, while the other occupants clung to the buggy. The horses swam across and pulled them to safety. Mother assured me that the new bridge would not go down, but I still felt breathless with apprehension as I heard the horses' hoofs hit the planks. The water lapped hungrily at the sand banks as if it wanted to pull something or somebody down. I offered a fervent, silent prayer begging the Lord to help us cross safely, then, back on the road, bowed my head again in gratitude. Dad's story, told many times, of three men drowned when their boat capsized a half mile west by the willow trees, added to my horror of water and hatred of Bear River.

We reached Benson Ward and passed the red brick schoolhouse with its high windows and the big rusty bell up in the tower. In the school yard was a big pole swing, two privies with hieroglyphics on the doors that I could not read from the road, and a straw shed for the ponies that were ridden to school.

Then came the overflow well and the public watering trough where Dad stopped and let the sweating team drink to their heart's content. When they slobbered and shook the hot harness, they were ready for the last lap of our journey.

Logan was straight east, a city with electric lights, a street car, and paved sidewalks! We could see the Agricultural College (A.C.) on the hill and the spire of the temple. We were not tired anymore. Too many sights and sounds awaited us. For instance, as we passed the coal yard with big piles of shiny, black fuel, Dad said that city folks bought coal any time of the year they wanted and didn't lay in a winter supply as we did.

We crossed the track, and followed the dusty road that wound around the utility poles to avoid the chuck-holes. Across the road was a horse-drawn milk wagon and a man with a basket full of bottles of milk putting one or two on each doorstep. We were awed as Dad explained that this was the way city people got their milk. Cows were not allowed in the city limits.

We passed the livery stable where horses and buggies could be hired, and we drove on down to the old tie yard. We got out of the buggy, stretched, and shook off the dust. Dad unbridled the horses and fed them the hay he had tied on the back of the buggy. He visited with other families who were doing the same thing. Their mothers, like ours, brought out towels, wash rags, and combs and proceeded to work us over. "We must not look like country jakes in the city," Mother said, giving each of us a fond stroke or pat.

Holding hands in a long row, like a skirmish line, we started uptown to do our shopping. Dad's favorite men's store was Newbold's, so we stopped there first and tried hats, shoes, and suits on the boys. Mr. Newbold had a clever way of bargaining, making Dad feel like patting himself on the back whether he made a good buy or not. Mother warned us not to finger the showcase or touch the ties.

At dinnertime, we went to our favorite Chinese restaurant on Center Street and crowded into one booth. What smells for hungry travelers! Then came the waiter with his sleek black hair and freshly starched white coat. Expressionlessly, he announced the menu: roast beef, roast pork, salmon, apple pie, raisin pie, and custard. Mother said, "Dad, these kids can't eat a full dinner. Perhaps we can divide one dinner between two of them."

Dad was a man of few words. He looked at the waiter and said, "Six orders of roast beef."

The waiter came with six steaming bowls of soup. A big bowl of oyster crackers sat in the middle of the table. I took so many, my soup became a thick paste. I ate it, having been taught that no food should be wasted. Mother pronounced the gravy "flat," so we all applied a generous sprinkling of salt, pepper, and a little catsup. There was a new kind of salad—cold lima beans with big slices of raw onion and a little vinegar. Mother murmured, "If you don't like it, you don't have to eat it." Last came the apple pie. It was not as good as Mother's, but we ate it, in the meantime enjoying the sound of the streetcar and the delivery wagons and the sight of so many people going up and down the sidewalk.

With dinner over, we continued shopping. About four o'clock as we wearied, there was another treat. Dad took us to Murdock's Candy Kitchen where we were allowed our favorite ice cream soda. What enchantment! The rich mahogany furnishings, all those chocolates in sparkling, clear showcases, and the smell of chocolate and candy! One of us kids, fascinated and gawking, knocked his soda on the floor and smashed the glass. Mother blushed. The clerk smiled, "Accidents will happen," and would take no payment for the glass. Dad bought a big sack of nut taffy to eat on the way home. Our feet ached, but we forgot them on our homeward journey, laughing and chatting over the events of the day.

As we neared the clay slough, Mother took a small, brown turban out of a sack and tried it on. Dad looked it over in his quiet way and, with eyes twinkling, said, "So you rode all the way to Logan for that." It was a crushing blow to Mother's pride as well as to her good taste. She crammed the hat back into the sack, and I never remember her wearing it.

For the next ten miles, no one spoke. The boys leaned their sweating heads together and somehow managed to sleep in an upright position, shifting now and then as we hit a rut. It was twilight. Suddenly, Mother forgot her wounded feelings and began to talk.

"I see the spell is broken," Father laughed slyly. He again began to make fun of the little brown hat, not realizing his banter would cost him the price of another one.

The kerosene lamps flickered as we drove down the hill back home. Mother hustled us children to bed while Dad unharnessed the team and unloaded the buggy. Exhausted and overjoyed, I lay in bed thinking of the navy blue scarf for my new dress, my first breast pin with glass sets, a new pair of buttoned shoes, and that new, blue satin bow for my old hat.

We had been to Logan!

## Oyster Crackers

The highlight of a trip to Logan for any Clarkstonite was dinner at a cafe. What mouth-watering ecstacy to smell the variety of foods; how important it made one feel to sit in a little secluded booth; and what exquisite delirium to hear the waiter rattle off mechanically, "Roast beef, pork, mutton stew or links." A real choice to make, all for thirty-five cents.

Aunt Hanner, a hard-working, blunt, outspoken woman, went to Logan, and of course she went to a cafe for dinner. There on the table was a big bowl of oyster crackers. She stirred all she could into her soup, but a half bowl remained. Being of a conservative nature, Aunt Hanner reasoned that she had paid for those crackers and could justly put the remainder in her purse. But she forgot to take her money out first. As she opened her purse to pay for her dinner, a white avalanche of little round crackers fell to the floor. Behind the counter, down the aisle, and under the stools, the little crackers rolled. Crackers! Little oyster crackers, and a blushing, stammering Aunt Hanner. Her two girls, who liked a good joke no matter who it was on, never let the oyster cracker story die.

## John and the Mule

John Shumway, who has a fine sense of humor, told this story on himself. He and his wife, Mame, had been to Clarkston visiting relatives and were returning to their home in Garland. For some reason, he and Mame were not on speaking terms. They jogged along in morbid silence until they came to an ugly jackass with his head hanging over the fence. John, teasing good-naturedly, asked, "Mame, could that jackass, by any chance be a relative of yours?"

Mame replied cunningly, "Only by marriage." Needless to say, their sulks were over, and they laughed heartily.

## Past Springs

Here are some newspaper clippings about Clarkston, yellowed with age, that I found pasted in my Grandpa Barson's old scrapbook.

### March 12, 1878

J.E. Carlisle, a school teacher writing from Clarkston, Utah:"The people of Clarkston feel thankful for the mild winter almost gone. The health of the community in general has been good. Clarkston can now boast a dramatic organization, Martin Harris, manager; Michael Clark, stage manager. On the night of the 23rd, they played the well known drama, *The Charcoal Burner,* followed by the farce of *Toodles.* Considerable talent was displayed; their acting will compare favorably with the older and more experienced companies."

### April 4, 1895

The farmers over this way are getting their farming utensils ready and some are already plowing on the highlands. The snow is going fast and the warm days make one thing certain—that spring has come at last.

Quite a number of our people lately are suffering with bad colds, but all are on the mend at present.

# Aunt Bessie's Wedding

"What will people say if you marry us, Father?" Aunt Bessie asked in a worried tone.

"And what do we care what people say?" replied Grandpa Barson tartly with that look of determination in his eye that announced he'd get what he wanted. Grandpa ruled his family with majesty and a lordly air, and even though we could not always agree with him, he gave us confidence and we fell in line to keep family peace.

"I am the justice of the peace," Grandpa chortled proudly. "I have the legal right to marry you, so why not? Nothing like this has ever been done in our little town. Let's give folks something to talk about. What do you say?" He whirled his derby on his cane as a final gesture, and Aunt Bessie, who had never disobeyed him in her life, knew her plans had been made for her. We did not remind him that he, a devout Mormon, had often remarked, "A civil ceremony did not amount to more than jumping over a damned broomstick."

Grandpa secretly obtained a copy of the marriage ceremony from the county courthouse and practiced it with all the dignity of a doctor of law. The morning of 23 April 1912 dawned in all its spring glory. Splotches of yellow daffodils were in full bloom, tulips were in bud, and tiny crocuses, filled with dew, lifted their cups to the morning sun. At 8:30 a.m., Phil Rasmussen, the nervous young bridegroom, appeared at the Barson home with his mother. Phil was decked out in a new brown suit with a matching tie and shoes and nervously wiped his brow as good mornings were said.

Bessie opened her mother's bedroom door lightly and came forward in a lavender delaine dress with a floral net overskirt edged with deep cream silk fringe. Her slippers were white satin with lavender laces. With her brown hair combed back in soft waves, she was a beautiful bride. Grandma looked at her baby girl, blushing and radiant, now about to leave her. She choked back the tears. They could wait until all were asleep that night.

Grandpa stood the young couple under the chandelier that had been decorated with white honeycomb wedding bells and read the ceremony with a flourish. After the "I do's," Phil kissed his bride; and Tommy Griffin, a neighbor, signed his name as a witness.

After the usual kissing and congratulations, the young couple walked to their new home just through the block to see that all was in readiness for housekeeping. Grandpa had already made a gate through the back fence, and a little path through the weeds showed that Aunt Bessie had already transported her trousseau: two quilts, three sheets, three pairs of pillow cases, two towel sets, a double blanket, two pie plates, two cake pans, an eggbeater, and a pancake turner.

The newlyweds looked over their possessions. There was a new black and shiny coal range, a round table, a sideboard as a present from Grandma, a dresser, a brass bedstead all made up, and home-made carpet on the floor. Everything was ready. "The day I'm married I'm leaving home," Aunt Bessie had resolved. "I'll not stay one night in my father's home." But she had no idea of the prank that was brewing.

Four o'clock came—time for the wedding dinner. The big table, spread the full length of the dining room, groaned with the bounties of the farm. There was roast chicken and dressing, mashed potatoes and gravy, relishes, pickles, dried corn, and homemade ice cream. Grandma had made the wedding cake, and Aunt Bessie had decorated it. The first table was for the grownups, then the dishes were washed and it was set again for the kids while the old folks visited in the parlor.

Then came the program. Aunt Effie sang and then, by popular request, gave an encore of the old favorite "We Are Growing Old Together." Uncle Hyrum played the fiddle and Aunt Bessie the piano while Grandpa led the quadrilles and marches over the floral rug on the parlor floor.

It was time then to open the gifts. The young couple sat in the middle of the floor and made wishes for the givers as they unwrapped each present—no modern crystal or gadgets, just plain everyday articles, such as a tin tub, a wash board, a flour sieve, a rolling pin, a water pitcher and bowl set, a framed picture of a bowl of fruit, a kerosene lamp, a broom, a dustpan, a floor mop, a sack of flour, ten pounds of sugar, a glass berry set edged with gold, a granite wash bowl, a quart tin cup, a fire shovel, a red-and-white checked tablecloth, a water bucket, a coal scuttle, a tea kettle, a china lamp, an unusual linen tablecloth, face towels, a netted doily, and a clock that chimed as a special gift from the choir where Aunt Bessie was organist. Any wedding was not complete unless someone sent a bedroom chamber pot half filled with root beer, and this one was no exception.

Unnoticed while all this gaiety was taking place, a few friends and relatives made their way to the Rasmussen cottage. Finding one window unlocked, they climbed through and took all the bedding to a sister's home. With delight, they tugged away the big feather bed, leaving only the bare springs.

When the party ended, the happy couple returned to their little nest. At first, they laughed and hunted through the hay stack and the chicken coop. One o'clock, two o'clock, three o'clock, and Aunt Bessie was still wandering in her white satin slippers and beautiful lavender gown. In tears she went back to Grandma's and woke her up. Grandma scolded over such a dirty trick and made them a bed on the hard davenport in the parlor. Grandpa laughed. He blamed no town hoodlums. He knew the guilty parties would be found in his own family. After all, he had taught them to enjoy a good joke.

## Traded Brides

When it came to marriage, a relative of mine was part of a true story in the early 1880's that was talked about in Clarkston from then on. Henry Yates showed a picture of Maria Pack and her seven children to George Godfrey, my first cousin, and Alfred Atkinson. "Notice these two girls, Ada and Lizzie," he said. "They will become second wives to any good man who will pay for their passage to America. I'll marry Maria as my second wife, but seven children are more than I can support. What do you say, brethren? They're nice-looking girls."

"I'll pay the fare for Ada," said George, looking intently at the picture, "And I'll marry her as soon as she comes."

"That takes care of one of them," laughed Henry. "Now how about you, Alfred? You know the Church advises you to have two wives."

"I'll take Lizzie, then," said Alfred a little hesitantly. "How much did you say that fare was?"

"You won't be sorry," consoled Henry. "They're a fine family. I know because I've seen them."

Some time later, Henry received word about when Maria and her family would be at Cache Junction. He hitched his team to the wagon and, with a light heart, went to meet her. In the meantime, he moved his first wife, Ann, into one room of the house to make room for Maria and her children. Poor Ann was almost crowded out to make room for another, but the Church said, "Practice polygamy. We'll show the government they can't stop us." And this was the result.

When Henry returned, George and Alfred were there to claim their mail-order brides. In the picture, Ada had seemed prettier; but face to face, Lizzie was downright beautiful. She was a small brunette with brown eyes and matching brown hair. George knew at once that he wanted her, not Ada, but how could he persuade Alfred? He called the second bridegroom aside and proposed a trade. Alfred, too, found Lizzie's beauty desirable, but good looks were not as important to him as they were to George. To him a second wife was important to bear children, work, and cook his meals. Whether any property entered the trade, no one ever knew, but George got the beautiful Lizzie.

George's first wife, Lizzie of German descent, was living in a house too small for another woman, so he built Lizzie II a little house on the corner. She was all that George could ask for—clean and neat, a good cook, and a lover of old England as he was. George and Lizzie II had a large family of eight children, and his first wife was often left to fend for herself.

Alfred built a small house for Ada a block east of his family home. Alfred and his first wife, Matilda, had nine children, but Matilda did not complain when Alfred married Ada. Ada bore but two children. Her health was not good, and she seemed quite unhappy. Later Alfred went to Canada and when he came back moved in with Ada, leaving Matilda on her own to make a living for her family. Amazingly, Matilda was never know to complain about *any* of her circumstances—not even then.

Ada and Lizzie were the oldest in Maria's family. The other five of Maria's children grew up and married. It was rumored that Maria's first husband, who could not accept the gospel in England, committed suicide after his wife and children came to America, but this is a matter of speculation. However, the story of the traded brides remains bright in Clarkston folklore.

# The Queen of the May

Clarkston always prided itself on its May Day celebration. Every year the town's most prominent bride-to-be was crowned Queen of the May by her prospective husband, who tenderly lowered a crown made of pasteboard covered with gold paper and trimmed with beads or spring flowers to her curls. As a little girl, I watched wide-eyed. This ancient English spring festival was the ultimate in romance and glamour.

But one particular year, Mother Nature failed to provide the flowers of spring. It was still damp and cold. The snow lay in such deep mounds on the foothills that the buttercups could not add their yellow touch of spring. Even the grass was a sickly, yellow color. But the committee assigned to organize the celebration went ahead in spite of the frosty reminders of winter.

Margaret Buttars was chosen queen and was to be crowned during the program by her fiancé. At nine o'clock, time for the parade and band concert, a black cloud settled directly above us, but no one took heed. The chosen queen, Margaret, sat on a throne in the center of a flat rack, decorated with yards of white bunting, drawn by two of the town's whitest horses, and driven by her fiancé, the King of the May. The queen's four attendants, dressed in starched white gowns, sat in each corner. The brass band broke forth into tunes we knew by heart. And then, perfectly timed, the snow began simultaneously with the parade. Thick white flakes fell on the band music, and notes ran into one inky blotch. The queen shivered on her throne; the maids, with chattering teeth, tried to wave and smile. The ladies' hair, that had been painstakingly curled in rags the night before, fell in damp strings around their faces, as winter came back for a final encore.

But the parade rolled on without a hitch until the clown band came by, with Joe Christensen playing "A Sweet Bunch of Daisies" on his accordion. His cow was hooked up with the horse on the little cart. The cow, irritated by the snow and the music, gouged the horse in the ribs. The horse gave a lunge, broke the tugs, and was gone. The clowns jumped out, but Brother Christensen dropped his accordion, which stretched out to its full length in the road. Before it could be retrieved, the cow made a backward plunge with the cart, cutting it in two. Clarkston's one and only accordion was gone. He dragged the cow away while the children on ponies rode by. New hair ribbons hung limp with snow, and saddle and bridle decorations shrank into wet wads of paper.

Undaunted by the sleet, a dozen little girls in new white May Day dresses began to braid the maypole. As they wound in and out, the wet crepe paper streamers stretched and finally broke, leaving stains of blue and red on the prized dresses.

The snow fell faster. The bright green leaves were soon covered with a dazzling white that bent the limbs of trees and bushes to the ground. "Do you think we ought to go home and call it off?" Brother Jenson asked the bishop, his teeth chattering in time to the music of the band.

"Didn't you cross the plains, Brother Jenson?" the bishop asked. "Did you go home when it snowed? Did a little storm stop the pioneers? No, and it shan't stop us!"

Warmed by the bishop's words, those around him took heart. The janitor, a practical man, brought in two big buckets of coal and wood from the little coal house and started a fire in the black, pot-bellied stove of the meeting house. Soon dark smoke was belching forth from the inside, as well as from the chimney, promising to dry our cold, wet clothes.

Shivering and bedraggled, the people entered the building. An array of bare-bottomed babies stretched their legs toward the heat as they welcomed dry diapers, then pressed their red noses against their mothers' breasts for a nourishing draught of warm milk.

Brother Keep shook the snow off his coat into the coal bucket. "We're all fools, that's what I say. We'll have a dose of pneumonia, and it will serve us right, it will. Celebratin' in a snow storm!"

"As your faith is, so shall it be, Brother Keep," rejoined another. "Look out of the window. Already the sun is shining through the clouds."

The heat from the stove poured forth, and the sun began to shine, sending little rivulets down the window panes. Spirits brightened as a girls' chorus burst into its ritual song:

> The glad May morn with its rosy light is breaking
> O'er the hills so lovely and fair.
> Then away, away, away,
> And away, away, away,
> And a Maying we will go.

The big moment arrived. The king got up and twirled the crown around on his fingers, praised the beauties of the month of May, and placed the crown upon his bride-to-be, the Queen of May.

In 1955 when Herman Thompson and Annie Jardine Thompson celebrated their fiftieth wedding anniversary, they still had the speeches they had read fifty years before when Herman had been a gallant King of the May and Annie H. Jardine had been a radiant queen. Herman's brother Herbert had written his speech:

> Ladies, gents, and friends, I am proud of the honor bestowed upon me this first day of May 1905. Of all the months of the year, this is indeed the most beautiful. This is the month when nature is clothed in all of

22

her lovely beauty. The mountains, hills, and valley are trimmed with growing grass, intermingled with the sweet fragrance of flowers.

> We honor three fair daisies all
> Fair roses, buds, and blossoms small.
> And ye, fair maiden of the day
> For now I crown you Queen of May.

A hundred thousand times I call a hearty welcome to you all. I love this merry season when all hearts swell with our joyous Queen. May it ever be so. And long live our Queen.

Hulda Thompson wrote the queen's speech for Annie Jardine that year:

> Our gallant king has crowned me queen,
> And all her maidens fair
> Have joined with us this balmy day
> To make it one so rare.
> And you, dear friends, who've come today
> To greet this new and merry May,
> May joyous fragrance fill the air
> And tune your hearts today.
> May birds and bees their silver notes
> Pour forth upon the air;
> And flowers' fragrance ever bloom
> To banish thoughts of care.
> May heavens's blessings on us all
> And on this happy day,
> Pour forth in gladness joy and song,
> This merry month of May.

Herman and Annie still remembered these moments of youthful glory when they celebrated their golden wedding anniversary in 1955.

# Uncle John's Funeral

It was 24 May 1910, when I was just ten years old, that

Uncle John died. He had been ill three weeks with spotted fever. As soon as he was pronounced dead, relatives and neighbors gathered and moved all of the bedroom furniture into the coal house. Then they carried in two saw-horses and enough boards to lay Uncle John out. The women cried and tried to comfort Aunt Jenny, and the men talked about all of the fine qualities of Uncle John as they packed ice into quart bottles to lay around his body. They tied a strip of cloth around his head to hold his jaws together and put coins on his eyelids to make them stay shut.

There was an undertaker in Logan, but people in our town said they wanted to go back to Mother Earth as God intended, with their bodies unmolested by any money-grabbing undertaker. They also preferred their homemade coffins. "Boughten" ones were cheap and shoddy compared with Clarkston's. Brother Thompson, the town carpenter, made all the coffins of our own native pine. He covered them with white plush if the family could afford it and outing flannel if they couldn't. The material was always kept on hand by the co-op store, but the silver handles and breast plate had to be shipped from Ogden. Sometimes when the train service was poor, wooden knobs had to be hastily substituted. Those who could pay Brother Thompson gave him what they saw fit, and he never charged a widow.

After Uncle John was laid out, men stayed night and day until time for the services, changing the ice and keeping wet cloths over his face. On the day of the funeral, Uncle John, dressed in white, was laid in his coffin, which was held by two chairs. There was no make-up, no soft lights, or flimsy veil. Everything was bold and glaring. What a ghastly sight dear Uncle John made! In spite of all the precautions, his left eye was slightly open and his mouth had fallen slightly ajar, showing some of his teeth. As I looked at him, a fear and horror of death came over me that I have never overcome.

As people passed the bier, they shook Aunt Jenny's hand and made the customary remark, "How fine he looks," but outside I heard them say, "Did you see that black spot on his cheek? It's good they didn't try to keep him any longer."

What an awful, gruesome experience death is, I thought as I stood outside watching people file in and out. Strangers shook hands with everyone, and relatives kissed and cried on each other's shoulders. The crowd cleared away as Aunt Jenny and her family kissed Uncle John goodbye. I didn't want to see this scene, but I could hear the sobbing and kept trying to swallow the big lump in my throat.

A white-top buggy with a white team and the town's best harness arrived to take the remains to the meeting-house. But Aunt Jenny said no. Uncle John had loved his bay team so much, wouldn't the driver please use them instead of the traditional team? After the change was made, the pallbearers put the coffin into the buggy. Aunt Jenny and her family rode in the buggy behind the coffin, and the relatives followed in order of age.

The organist was playing, "Nearer, My God, to Thee" as we entered the building. The congregation remained standing until all the mourners were seated. The Relief Society president arranged the flowers on the casket with meticulous care. There were two bunches of lilacs, some yellow tulips, purple "flags," and a bunch of red paper flowers.

The choir sang "Shall We Meet Beyond the River?" One speaker dwelt on the glories of the resurrection. Another spoke of Uncle John's mission in heaven and asked the blessings of the Lord on Aunt Jenny and her family. They all said so many fine things about Uncle John that I wondered if they were talking about the spunky, temperamental fellow I had known in the flesh.

But dead people are perfect, so I chided myself and resolved never again to remember one unkind thing about Uncle John. The choir sang, "God Be With You Till We Meet Again." As we marched out, people wiped their eyes and watched Aunt Jenny intently to see just how hard she was taking it.

The funeral procession then lined up and drove out to the graveyard on the hill. There were fifteen white-top buggies, two black buggies drawn by single horses, and one wagon in the cortege. When we reached the graveyard, the horses were tied to posts along the barbed wire fence. Only the buggy with the coffin drove in where a deep hole awaited the remains. The pallbearers steadied the coffin and lowered it with two ropes down into a rough plank box. Then a nimble little fellow went down into the grave by means of a rope and put on the lid. People gathered round with bowed heads, and an awed silence crept over all. Just as the dedication prayer was being said, a screaming flock of seagulls flew over, lighting in the freshly plowed ground just through the fence. They continued their piercing dirge until the prayer was finished. Their cries were as chilling as a winter's night. No one moved. Four men with shovels began the slow task of filling in the grave. Thud, thud went the dirt as it covered Uncle John. A little breeze fanned the scent of the wild, sweet williams through the air. "Thud, Thud" continued the dirt. No one spoke. The awful silence was broken by a horse as it pawed in the soft earth and pulled back against a creaking barbed wire fence. Four other men took the place of those who had been working with the shovels. I watched the lizards crawling around the headstones and the shinebacked stink bugs that ran around our feet. The dirt in the grave was getting higher now. One man put a piece of cedar post at the head of the grave and a smaller one at the foot as the dull shoveling continued. The grave was finally finished and patted into a smooth mound with the shovel backs.

People then began walking around the graves of their own loved ones. I read the epitaph I liked best:

Sleep, Mother dear,
And take your rest.
God called you home.
He thought it best.

I could never understand why God needed this mother more than her own children did, but such was the faith of my forefathers. Whatever happened was God's will, and God's will was always best.

The graveyard seemed crawling with animal life. Ant hills with their swarming colonies were everywhere, and gopher holes, of an undetermined depth, were by most of the graves. I hated the thoughts of gophers molesting the body, but Mother always said, "When the spirit leaves the body, the person is gone and the body goes back to dust anyway, so nothing that happens to the body matters." I still hated the thoughts of these little creatures gnawing away to speed up nature's process.

With the passing of time, the old Clarkston graveyard has changed. The dried, matted clumps of purple "flags," the briar roses, the lilac bushes, and the lone locust tree are only memories. A plush carpet of green covers the ant hills, and the lizards and beetles have moved on or died off. The lonely hill has become a place of beauty. Sometimes I look at the spot where my weary bones will eventually lie, and then I chill and stiffen as that awful childhood fear of death returns. I see Uncle John with his partly open eye and the ghastly look upon his face. Death is not the sweet, solemn thought spoken of by the poet, but it is the only way out. "Dust thou art, and to dust thou shalt return."

# Aunt Matilda

Every morning in spring and summer when I awoke, I could hear the scritch-scratch of a hoe. It was Aunt Matilda waging war on the mustard and marshmallow weeds in her garden. She liked to sing as she loosened the rich, black loam around each plant.

I thus woke up feeling that the world was a lovely place and peeked out to see Aunt Matilda as she worked in her garden. What a world of beauty she created around her. Her log house was covered with Virginia creeper, and the ugly pole fence was hidden by yellow roses, lilacs, and hollyhocks. It was an array of splendor from the early daffodils of spring to late chrysanthemums in the fall. Every Sunday morning, Aunt Matilda could be seen on her way to church carrying a bouquet for the pulpit. She brought flowers into every sickroom and generously shared flowers with her friends, too. She was like Johnny Appleseed—not with fruit, but with flowers. Hollyhocks grew along fences and butterballs thrived on wet ditch banks, all because Aunt Matilda had been there with her little bag of seeds.

To call on Aunt Matilda meant hearing choice bits of poetry from Church magazines as well as the classics. She loved to recite Tennyson's "Crossing the Bar" to the grownups and "Little Orphan Annie" to the kids.

Then you had to see the latest painting that she and her girls had done, hung up to dry in the back room. There were black sateen pillow tops decorated with swans and water lilies, and some with peacocks with fancy tails glowing with every hue. There were wall decorations with "God Bless Our Home" painted on them, and waist aprons with cross-stitch designs.

I was always invited to share their frugal meals. For supper there was bread and milk, honey in the comb, raw vegetables in season, and chokecherry jelly. Not fancy, but nourishing. Anyone calling at mealtime was welcome.

There was always the same smell in Aunt Matilda's home—a conglomeration of drying herbs, oil paints, seeds and apples out to dry, and old books and newspapers. Aunt Matilda was unperturbed in the midst of it all. With her hair combed in two braids wrapped around her head, a red blouse, a black skirt, and a checked waist apron, Aunt Matilda was a model of serenity. Life had not always been good to her, but she filled her cup with so much that was good and worthwhile that there was no room left for bitterness. She was an angelic soul who made the desert bloom.

## Church Meetings

Clarkston Ward in its early days practiced the Churchwide custom of extemporaneous preaching. The bishop would stand up and call a man (women were exempt) to the pulpit without any prior warning, based on the theory that every elder in the Church had a testimony of the truthfulness of the gospel and would promptly obey any call from someone in authority.

That was the theory. The practice provided some harrowing stories. Uncle Tom Griffin and Uncle Tom Godfrey could always be relied upon for an entertaining, extemporaneous speech; but they were the two exceptions. When Uncle Al was called upon to speak, he turned pale, stood up, and said curtly, "I don't belong to this outfit," and walked out. At another meeting, a young man called on to give the closing prayer, muttered audibly, "The old sons-of-b—," but obediently dismissed the meeting.

On this particular spring day, sacrament meeting convened as usual on Sunday at 2 p.m. My friend and I marched up the carpeted aisle and took a seat near the front, our legs dangling over the edge of the splintered bench. The choir and congregation sang "Guide Us, O Thou Great Jehovah," and Brother Bengt Ravsten was called upon to give the opening prayer. Stiff with rheumatism, he climbed the three steps to the stand with difficulty, raised both hands high above his head, and in broken Swedish, invoked the blessings of the Lord upon us. The choir sang something about Jesus' name and the sacrament was blessed. The big silver goblet of water started down our row, first to Sister Yates, and next to her retarded son who had a runny nose. One lady farther down deftly wiped a clean spot on the rim with her hanky. We nudged each other and wished we dare do the same when it came to us.

The first speaker was Brother Charley Anderson. I couldn't understand his broken language, so I began looking around for something more entertaining. There were the green, glass gooseberries on Aunt Minnie's hat that always fascinated me and the pink bird on Aunt Emma's. Grandma had a small black hat with a black feather, and I was wondering how old it was when my friend elbowed me. "Look," she whispered. "See that bedbug crawling on that man's collar?" Up, down, over, and under it crawled. We giggled, and a sharp look from Mother told me to stop whatever we were having fun about.

Brother Anderson finished and Bishop Jardine said, "Brother Zeke, will you please come up and talk to us?" Brother Zeke was not disposed. He turned red and walked out of the meeting. "Brother Zeke is just a little afraid," said the bishop. "Brother Denny, you go and persuade him to come back and bear his testimony." Brother Denny went but did not return.

"We lost Brother Zeke and now we've lost Brother

Denny," the bishop acknowledged, then sternly proceeded to remind us of the judgments of God that would fall upon those who refused to testify of his goodness. He then announced a special meeting held on Thursday at which some in the ward who had sinned would ask forgiveness. My friend and I decided to go, even though we had heard that at these meetings many people cried, especially the women. Embarrassing, but intriguing just the same.

The choir sang another song that impressed me with the words "Rise to judgement, rise to judgment," and we were dismissed.

At the appointed time on Thursday, we were on the same slivery bench. The meeting began with prayer and Grandpa Barson was called to the stand. Bishop Jardine said, "Brother Barson, you have been found guilty of working on the sabbath."

"Yes," Grandpa replied, "I thought my ox was in the mire. My grain was ripe and this was the only day I could borrow Hans Dahle's sickle."

"Ox or no ox," stormed the fiery little bishop, "Latter-day Saints do not break the sabbath day. You have admitted your guilt. Now ask these brethren and sisters to forgive you."

"I ask you to forgive me," said Grandpa in a matter-of-fact manner, showing no signs of repentance. Knowing my Grandpa, that twinkle in his eye told me he didn't mean a word of it and would work again on Sunday if he thought it was necessary.

Brother Thompson then asked forgiveness for misreading his water notice and taking Sister Atkinson's water. By show of hands, he was unanimously forgiven.

Sister Mary took the stand and said she had borne false witness. I didn't know what that was and neither did my friend, but we raised our hands with the rest to forgive her.

Then Dick and Sarah stood up together. Sarah was crying, Dick put his arm around her bashfully but protectively, and all of the women began to bawl. Sarah said through her sobs that she had sinned and hoped everyone would forgive her. What did she mean? We could see she was expecting a baby, but Mormons liked children. Then Dick's chin began to quiver, he got all choked up, and finally he stammered that he'd sinned and would people forgive him? Sarah was crying hard now and so were the women. The men just swallowed, shuffled their feet, and looked stern. Everyone raised their hands to forgive these two, as well, and meeting was dismissed. Then the people shook hands, sinners and all, and went home.

My friend and I turned somersaults out on the log poles along the hitching posts for awhile. We agreed on hoping we'd never do a thing to ask forgiveness for. That would sure be an awful feeling, up there on the stand with people looking at you, and you a-bawlin'. We looked at the sun and saw that it was close to Old Gunsight on the west mountains—time to scamper off and bring the cows from the meadows.

## Visitors from the Other Side

A good standing joke is told on one of our bishops. Meetings announced for Clarkston's two-story meetinghouse always designate the location as "above" or "below." Our stake headquarters were located on the east side of the valley, commonly called, in Clarkston, "the other side." One night our bishop announced, "We will meet up above tonight. We are expecting visitors from the other side."

# Section II

# Summer

*Summer was sapphires—the rich blue of the clear sky above and the blue water.*

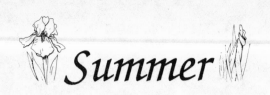

# Summer

Summer meant fishing. On the day of this treat, Dad would cut down willows along the river bank to make a rod for each one of us. We threaded our hooks on our twine line, tied on a bolt or bur for a sinker, and dug in the garden for plenty of angleworms to lure the carp and suckers in. If gnats and mosquitoes became too numerous and nibbles on our line too few, we set our poles on a forked stick and ran off to play.

From the river meadows, we could see the train come out of Bear River Canyon and wind along the hill, high above the river. The engineer always waved back when we waved. We could see real people on the train. Where might they be coming? And why?

For dinner, we had crisp fish cooked over an open bonfire sometimes burned, sometimes rare, but always good.

Then in the long, lazy afternoon of more fishing came a sense of endless security, of slow-moving hours with Dad close by and brothers fishing on either side of me. The sun burned through my bonnet. The warm, wet clay oozed through my toes. The soft lapping of the water would be broken now and then by the call of a killdeer or the thud of horses' hoofs and wagon wheels as someone drove over the old wooden bridge.

August brought garnets and amethysts. It meant chokecherry time, our annual trip to Cold Water Canyon to gather fruit for our winter's jelly and to enjoy a picnic. After eating chokecherries until our mouths were stained and puckered, we filled our buckets with the ripe, purple fruit. One brother would straddle the limb to hold it down while we stripped off its fruit.

Sometimes, the tree retaliated. A crashing of branches! A chorus of "Look out!"

34

"Help! Here I come." And he would come banging down through the trees, his bucket of chokecherries rolling away down the hill like marbles. When we saw he wasn't hurt, the mountain echoed with our laughter. "Couldn't stick a branch," we teased, but he rubbed his scratches and looked half-bewildered, half-incensed.

For diversion, we found sea shells on the hill and listened as Mother told us again the story of Lake Bonneville. Our picnic dinner was bread and butter, canned salmon, lettuce from the garden, mustard pickles, and cake with the flaky frosting that flew away as we tried to take a bite.

## Our Street

Our street was lined on both sides with kids. There were the Ravstens with six, the Christensens with fifteen, the bishop's family with eleven, the Barsons with four, the Griffins with nine, and our own family of eight. All of us felt loved and wanted. Each new arrival was an asset.

Ours was a street of friendly hellos, stick horse brigades, burdock leaf hats and hollyhock dolls, mumble peg on the ditch banks under the crooked box elder trees, and ball games out in the road. Occasionally, we held meetings by the fence lines, solemnly imitating our elders. Our favorite song at these meetings was a little ditty that Aubry Griffin got somewhere and taught us. It ran:

> Bark at Mary,
> Robus a whistling
> Calling Smileo to the plow.
> See the little Rover dog run after.
> Join in the chorus, bow-wow-wow.

I've never heard this little air since, so I surmise there was a little originality attached to it. We warbled on hot summer nights until the call for bedtime came.

I played with rag dolls there, trimming cabbage leaf hats with chicken feathers and little yellow Johnny-jump-ups that grew along the sidewalk. The boys teetered along on stilts—wooden ones or tin cans tied to their feet with binder twine. In the evenings, we played "Hide and Seek" and "Run, Sheep, Run." Industriously we played baseball, fashioning our balls from worn-out woolen stockings and covered with soft leather from old shoes.

Monday was wash day on our street, come rain, hail, or wind. As I turn on my automatic washer, I think back to "blue Mondays" when I missed school to help do the family wash. We lugged and tugged the Western washer up from the cellar. In the summer, we put it under the box-elder tree in the dooryard, and in the winter it sat in the middle of the kitchen floor. We carried water from the well and heated it in a boiler over the kitchen range. My job was to cut the hard, homemade soap and take out bits of lean meat that hadn't dissolved in the soap-making process. Once melted, it would lather; but more often the undissolved bits clung to the clothes, and I was reprimanded for not shaving it finer. After the water heated, we poured it into the washer, and I began to turn the crank, my eyes glued to the clock. Each batch was turned fifteen minutes, and I don't believe I ever made an extra revolution.

The white clothes were then boiled; from the boiler, they went into the tub where Mother took the remaining dirt out with the scrubbing board. The last stage was the bluing. We rinsed and wrung and, with aching backs and arms, dropped the clothes into the basket ready for the clothes line, a wire strung from the swing pole to the poplar tree by the front gate. Then there was the dirty water to empty, and more water to bring in for the colored clothes.

In winter, steam dripped from the walls and masked

the windows. Mother would take off her glasses and put them in a dish in the cupboard; then she would lift her waist apron and wipe the sweat that ran down her face, singing all the while. Work to her was joy and never drudgery, and I caught that spirit being with her. The smell of baking potatoes and navy beans with salt pork kept up my morale until noon. After enjoying them with plenty of homemade bread and butter, we resumed our washing which lasted well into the afternoon. After the last batch was finished, there were endless buckets of water to empty, the washer, tubs and boiler to carry back to the cellar, and the floor to scrub.

Even though it meant taking extra exams for being absent from school, I was never sorry I helped my mother, for she was always my ideal of all that was fine and good. But who says those were the "good old days"? My back aches when I think of them.

I remember each Monday, in each yard, various sizes of overalls, long-handled underwear, thick black stockings, diapers, flour sacks, bloomers, and Mother Hubbard aprons waved in the breeze. One or two of the clotheslines in our little town always bore the calico "wrapper" that women wore during the last three months of pregnancy. These were many yards around, requiring at least an hour to iron, and so full they made these mothers look like a walking display of goods.

We children learned to revere motherhood by how mothers were treated. During the ten-day stay in bed that accompanied the birth of each little one, we older children carried such choice food as fried chicken, cream cake, Danish soup, and currant pie up, down, and across the street.

# Bringing in the Mail

About 11 a.m. every morning but Sunday, Johnny Burt, with a sweating team of wiry little bays hooked to a white-top buggy, brought in the mail. He made the trip daily to Cache Junction, eight miles away, through blizzards, mud, or summer heat. Anyone who needed to catch the train rode out with him, and any salesman or visitor rode in. It was twenty-five cents a ride if you felt like paying, and you were welcome if you didn't. Johnny was a genial little fellow.

Whenever we heard the rattle of Johnny's buggy, we peeped out to see if there was a passenger. What anticipation there was when we heard, "It's the music teacher today."

"It's the Jewish book peddler."

"It's somebody I've never seen before! He has two big suitcases."

We all felt a tinge of disappointment when we heard, "There's nobody today, just Johnny."

From Monday through Saturday, Sister Yates, a little Englishwoman who lived at the end of the block, walked to the post office with her little cloth mail bag and brought it back to deliver mail to each house up and down the street, stopping to chat a few minutes in each home. She always wore a gray shawl, the same shade as her hair, fastened about her shoulders with a large safety pin. A white scarf was tied under her chin.

The women always welcomed Sister Yates. It was a respite for her from her cross, ailing husband, groaning with the pains of rheumatism, and from the demands of her mentally retarded son. I think these visits with other women contributed to the cheerful brightness for which she was so well known.

Sister Yates had long ago lost all of her teeth and she always made me think of some lines by Oliver Wendell Holmes that I read in school:

> And now her nose is thin
> And rests upon her chin
> Like a staff.
> A crook is in her back
> And a melancholy crack
> In her laugh.

(I substituted "her" for "him" in the poem to make it fit Sister Yates.)

Faithful as the Pony Express through the blizzards of January or the sweltering heat of August, Sister Yates never failed to deliver the mail.

Tuesday was ironing day. The clothes were dampened on Monday night. Early Tuesday morning, the fire in the kitchen range was carefully made up. While the irons heated on the top, practical housewives killed two birds with one stone by baking bread. All up and down the street, the appetizing smell of fresh bread poured out of each torrid kitchen. If the meat wagon from Logan had arrived, the savory scent of our weekly roast or beefsteak would also drift out. Now and then, children would wander out the door, smacking their lips over freshly baked cookies or jelly tarts.

In summer, loads of hay went by, rolling up huge clouds of dust. Boys and girls taking cows to and from the pasture loitered along our sidewalks. Morning and night, Grandma Barson came out with her stick to hurry along the cows that stopped to snatch a bite of her golden glow or leave a steaming cowpie on her little patch of cement.

In the winter, we had the best street for coasting in town. Old and young came with bob sleighs and hand sleighs to line up at the top of the block and push off for a gleeful ride to the bottom. Sometimes the riders were piled three high on a sled, and the bottom one, whose job it was to steer, became confused under his load and piled them all in the snow bank. No one was ever seriously hurt, but a driver with a team and sleigh had to move cautiously through the small fry.

Big loads of wheat went down our street in the fall. At our corner, the drivers had to stop and apply the hand brake, giving some of the boys a chance to jump on and ride to the end of the block. As they rode, they scooped a handful of the new wheat into their mouths and chewed it into a delicious wad of gum that bulged both cheeks.

The street was the axis of my world, a safe world, a good world.

## Annual Peddlers

"The Watkins man has come to town," was always a pleasant cry on our street for it meant a free chew of gum for every child and the thrill of seeing that tall peddler open his two big suitcases. One contained flavoring and spices; the other contained mustard ointment, liniment, shampoo, and various kinds of salves and corn cures. Everyone bought from the Watkins man in spite of the ecclesiastical admonition to trade only at the co-op store. Mother's purchases always included a large bottle of vanilla, a can of cinnamon, and a bottle of that stinking liniment that we used on the sore joints and bellyaches of both man and beast.

As the peddler left our house, we followed him like the Pied Piper on down to the Griffins, but by the time he reached Grandpa Barson our ranks dwindled. Grandpa had a tongue like a razor, and he had trained us all to scamper like mice to their holes when a peddler reached his place. We sauntered up and down the sidewalk and just guessed what Grandpa bought.

It usually took the Watkins man about three days to canvass our town. He stayed at Sister Jardine's and paid for his board with his products. Then with an empty buggy and a well-filled purse, he started back for Logan. We all liked the Watkins man and looked forward to his coming.

Old Pete peddled fruit. He came into town in a covered wagon drawn by three horses. Most of our wagons needed only two horses, and the odd horse always looked in the way, but he was there without fail. Old Pete had a fine sales pitch, too. He was always overloaded and would have to sell at a loss to ease the burden on his horses. Dad could never resist water-melon, so he bought several, only to learn from another peddler a few days later that he had paid too much. Dad would call Old Pete some uncomplimentary names and say he would never buy from him again; but when Pete returned the next week, Dad bought more. Pete's melons had such a good flavor.

And I must not forget the meat man. Bell Brothers of Logan sent a meat wagon into Clarkston during the summer months. It had a large box with a double rear door built on the back of a buggy. Inside were blocks of ice to keep the meat cold, while a pair of scales hung from a chain just inside the doors. As the meat man entered town, he would begin ringing his bell. At the familiar sound, housewives dropped everything, grabbed straw hats or sunbonnets, and converged on the wagon from every direction with big tin pans and purses to get first choice of the steak. It was a welcome change from our daily ration of salt pork.

Besides steak and soup bones, he had minced ham and baloney which we gobbled by the slice without bread, standing right there in the road.

A mild-mannered little man with a long mustache curled on the ends made a semi-annual visit to our town bringing books. He was known to all as the "Cry Man" because he wept in every home. Whether there was gratitude in his heart for the gift of living or whether he thought tears helped his sales we never knew, but every visit was briny. He supplied almost every home with an almanac, *Hurlbut's Bible Stories,* and Dr. Gunn's book of cure-all remedies. Some dared to buy novels, although novel reading was severely frowned upon in our town. To be a novel-reader was a mark of an idle daydreamer, and laziness was a sin second only to dishonesty, so the book peddler was a little more practical. Wit and humor books sold readily and we all knew the latest jokes.

Another peddler who made semi-annual visits to Clarkston was a plump, dark lady who said she came from Syria. She rode into town with the mailman in his white-top buggy. He always stopped on our corner and helped the lady get out over the buggy wheels. Her long skirts were always in the way, and anyway, she lacked the knack. After he had her safely on the ground, he lifted out her two crammed suitcases.

Again we were first for a visit. She always arrived about noon, so she would trade Mother a pair of cheap, black stockings for her dinner. Then came her sob story. She would tell us how her two little children were waiting in Syria for her to get enough money to bring them to this country. If she could only sell enough, she could soon get them over here. The tears ran from her large, round, brown eyes as she told her story and opened her suit-cases. What a conglomeration they contained: stockings, hair pins, hat pins, combs, perfume, brooches, piece goods, and a few books of Bible stories.

Her sad, sad story never failed to touch Mother's loving heart, and she usually wound up buying several pieces of goods she didn't need or like, and some extra pairs of black stockings. I remember one purple dress of coarse material I had to wear, all because of those two little children in Syria. I often wonder whether they ever reached this country or not. Anyway, their so-called mother did a flourishing business in Clarkston on their account.

Louie, the junk man, always came to town in the spring. He drove a team of slow bays on a three-bed wagon and, for a few pennies, bought our old boots, leaking copper boilers and tea kettles, hides, beeswax, and iron from broken implements. We never could figure out what he did with this worthless rubbish, but he must have made money because he kept coming back. One day my small brother sold him Dad's good boots for a nickel. Dad was furious when he came home and gave us all several verses of "You should have known better," besides using all the adjectives that described Louie as a dishonest junk man. After he relieved his emotions, he took the boy and found Louie. The nickel and the boots changed hands.

Traveling high-powered shysters did not pass by Clarkston's most prosperous farmers with their sizable bank accounts. These con artists promised quick riches to the fortunate few who could invest right now. We heard about rubber stock in the plantations of South America or stock in bananas in some far-away land. When the farmers realized they had been robbed, they vowed to get even with these would-be benefactors. But of course they were never seen again. The next salesmen were treated coldly. The experienced among them noted the gleam in the eyes of those little groups of men gathered at the post office or store and usually got out while the getting was good.

The Watkins man today is the lone survivor of the peddlers of bygone days. The other night, one called on me, and as I looked over his wares, I noticed that old familiar scent compounded of liniment, cinnamon, and vanilla. Suddenly I was a little girl again, following a tall

Watkins man down a dirt sidewalk odiferous with wild
spearmint along the ditch bank, while all the children in
the neighborhood chewed gum.

## Past Summers

I found these yellowed clippings in my Grandpa
Barson's scrapbook of reports he had written, under the
name of Sanko, for the Logan *Journal.*

### On 27 June 1904:

Once more our little community is called upon to
mourn; this time the death of a beloved sister, Jane,
wife of Joseph Christensen, who departed this life
Friday morning, June 24. Sister Christensen was but
twenty-nine years of age, dying before the sun of her
life had reached its meridian, of troubles incident to
childbirth. She left a baby boy ten days old, a little girl
of three, a loving husband and a host of relatives and
friends to mourn her loss. She realized her end was
approaching and just before her death invited those
present to join her in singing "O My Father," which
they did, Sister Jane's voice leading clear and sweet.
She was highly esteemed in this community for her
many virtues.

Funeral services over her remains were held in the
meeting house Sunday afternoon at two o'clock,
memorial services for A. O. Woodruff being held
jointly. Counselor Thomas Griffin presided and
Elder Andrew Heggie offered the opening prayer.
During the services the choir sang beautiful selec-
tions. The speakers were Elders Bengt Ravsten,
James Jardine, Alex Archibald, Thomas Godfrey,
William Jensen of Newton, Bishop Ravsten, Ole
Petersen and Counselor Griffin, and well did they
offer words of comfort and consolation to the
bereaved. Elder P. S. Barson pronounced the

benediction. The family cortege embraced thirty-eight carriages, and when the cemetery was reached, Bishop Ravsten dedicated the last earthly resting place of our beloved sister.

### 14 June 1928:

A heavy hailstorm swept over the south side of Clarkston Tuesday, killing young chickens, destroying gardens and covering the ground to a depth of two inches.

July 2, Clarkston will have an old time Fourth celebration with a program, but the main feature will be a baseball game between the town's Cache Valley league and the thirty-eighth infantry of Fort Douglas.

# The Fourth of July

Clarkston summers were punctuated by its two important celebrations, the Fourth of July and Pioneer Day on the Twenty-fourth of July. For them, the whole ward gathered at Round Knoll, Steele's Canyon, or just down in the meadows for an afternoon and evening of a program, games, and eats. Of course, house parties, birthday surprises, quiltings, weddings, and political rallies occurred year-round.

The Fourth of July was enlivened by a parade. A Goddess of Liberty and two attendants rode on a hay rack trimmed with red, white, and blue bunting and small flags. The brass band was always on hand with the national anthem; and clowns, who had often had a spirited drink, added gaiety to the occasion. A home-grown orator extolled the founding fathers of our country. Then we had a program, dancing, and races for all. Whether our patriotism was aroused or not, I cannot say, but I do know it was a welcome break.

# The Twenty-fourth of July

Here is how Grandpa Barson (Sanko) reported the Twenty-fourth of July celebration in 1892. If it has a certain resemblance to our May Days and our Fourth of Julys, well, that's the way Clarkston liked its programs.

Our program was lengthy, with everyone responding to the call. The flag was raised at sunrise on the morning of the 24th by Captain William Jensen's Company and a salute of 20 guns was fired. At 9 o'clock our Brass Band serenaded the town. The wagon was pulled by four horses and beautifully decorated with red, white, and blue. John Dahle and Willard Archibald were the drivers. The music sounded sweet and helped to make everyone happy.

At ten o'clock a meeting was held in the Meeting House with Mr. Charles Shumway in charge. The choir sang an anthem, the prayer was given by Joseph E. Myler. The band broke forth with some more sweet strains. Our worthy bishop gave a short and spicy oration, followed by a song by Adam Fife.

Brother Richard Godfrey talked on the life of President Brigham Young. A song was sung by Mr. and Mrs. John P. Clark, followed by a 10 minute talk by Captain Yates on our Indian troubles. A select piece followed on the organ by Michael J. Clark. This brother was called out a second time. As George Godfrey had killed a nice fat beef and had sold it all before sunrise, all present were rejoicing over a good dinner.

A children's dance was held at 2:00 p.m. At four o'clock Thomas Buttars and Adam Fife had ten head of the best horses in town to run races, five horses on each side. Mr. Fife won the first prize for the first two races, and Mr. Buttars looked kinda sad, but the scale turned and Mr. Buttars won the last three races.

At five o'clock more fun commenced with Hans Larsen and Daniel Buttars choosing nine men on a side for a tug-of-war. The rope was stretched and

John Thompson gave the word of command. One hundred and twenty-three was counted and good pulling done, Hans Larsen winning two dollars. The side that lost did not feel satisfied and they pulled a second time. This time Daniel Buttars' side won a cash prize of eight dollars, which made them smile. These people were real sports.

The following named gentlemen have been asked to work on a committee to help sponsor a County Fair: Bishop John Jardine, Peter S. Barson and John Godfrey.

Well, I will close wishing you success. —Sanko

## Herbs and Plasters

Many people in our town openly mistrusted doctors, relying instead on herbs, patent medicines, and most important, the healing power of the Lord. With these three, they felt sustained in any emergency. Most cupboards contained consecrated olive oil, castor oil, Epsom salts, senna leaves, vermifuge, canker medicine, and Ward's liniment. That was enough for anyone.

It was probably a good thing that most of our people didn't believe in doctors. We couldn't get one anyway. The nearest doctors were at Logan, and in those days of bad roads and buggies, it took a mighty fine steed to make the trip. Then, too, doctors were considered an expensive luxury that no struggling farmer could afford. Our ancestors crossed the plains without medical help, so we considered ourselves weaklings not worthy of our heritage if we didn't get along likewise.

Perhaps some of these remedies seem foolish to us in these days of sulfa and myacins, but I wonder if we, under like conditions, could have done any better. Looking back, many of our remedies still seem quite sensible. However, some of our "old wives' tales" were not. For instance, women held the solemn belief that washing their hair during menstruation would surely cause death. Every mother whispered to her daughters the story of Annie, who failed to obey this rule and died. The belief was so firmly implanted in me that when my own daughters came along and scoffed at the story I could hardly let go. They brought me magazine articles, their physical education teachers told me tactfully that the story belonged to a passing age, and finally my own doctor told me my fears were groundless. I reluctantly decided that poor Annie died of something else. At any rate, there were loving hands to administer all our home treatments, and that love may have made up a large part of the therapy.

Olive oil was the most used medicine of my community. It was consecrated by the elders of the Church for the healing of the sick and was found in every home. People used it in spiritual therapy. The patient was anointed with it and then administered to by the elders. It was taken as a cure for appendicitis. Mixed with a few grains of sugar, it was given for coughs and croup. Combined with a few drops of camphor, it followed the stinging mustard plaster. It relieved sunburn and scratches, was applied to the scalp for dandruff, and was mixed with soda into a paste for severe burns.

Bishop Ravsten said at the bedside of one sick patient, "I feel prompted to oil the bowels." An olive oil enema was given. The result I remember was that the syringe was ruined.

Epsom salts was our stand-by as a physic. Salts were given daily for those suffering with spotted fever.

For infection, bread and milk poultices were used. When my Grandma Barson had an infection in her arm, she decided to try a cure she had only heard about— fresh cow manure. Grandpa obligingly brought some from the barnyard, and she bound her arm up in the stinking stuff. It didn't kill her.

Grandma also suffered from quinsy. She would have

the family catch frogs and put the legs on her throat. She became nervous from suffering so long with this disease and, at one time, used music for a sedative. She had Uncle Bird play the G chord on the organ over and over again until the monotony lulled her to sleep.

My aunt Vilate had a remedy for every ill. She never invoked the help of the Almighty when she could find something herself that would do the trick. And Doctors! She wouldn't give those conniving fellows any of *her* hard-earned money, and did her best to discourage others from giving theirs. In the fall, she gathered catnip from the ditch bank, carefully dried it, tied it in small bunches and hung it on the ceiling logs in the old cellar. There it remained for any emergency. When anyone called on her with a crying baby, she knew at once it had colic, and out came the catnip for tea. To save offense the babies were held down and drenched with this favorite remedy. If it did no good, at least it did no harm, for I never heard of a casualty from my aunt's catnip tea.

She made plasters of lard and mustard for chest colds, and I still shiver as I think of one being slapped on my chilling anatomy. She gave kerosene for croup. "It would cut the phlegm," she said. Thank heaven I was never stricken with croup while I stayed with her. But better still, she believed that a little bag of asafetida worn round the neck would ward off a cold. It should really ward off anything or anybody. The smell of garlic and onion mixed with b.o. was deadly indeed.

Of all her remedies, epsom salts was her favorite. She administered two big, heaping teaspoons to my cousins and me every Friday night. My aunt argued that if the house should be cleaned on Saturday so should the body, and without back talk our little bodies were thoroughly cleansed. She could put up a convincing defense for the bitter stuff. "Salts would flush the kidneys," she said. "They would cleanse the intestines of all the impurities," and above all, "they would purify the blood."

I was just at that greasy, pimply stage, and I felt that my blood needed purifying; and though nauseated by every dose, I took my salts with only a silent protest.

Besides all the physical benefits mentioned, Aunt Vilate was very keen. She knew there would be no drooping in bed for an extra hour of Saturday sleep. I lived at her house in Logan for four years while I attended high school (there was no high school in Clarkston) and graduated from B.Y. College. Every Saturday, without fail, the rumbling in my stomach brought me up an hour early. As I dashed downstairs, I would find my aunt with a piece of kindling braced from her stomach against the kitchen range. With the butcher knife, she would make little wood curls fly for the morning fire. With a knowing twinkle in her eye she always greeted me with "Are you up for the day?" Without comment, I grabbed the first coat I could find and departed. By night there was a well-beaten path to the old outhouse and the size of the Montgomery Ward Catalogue had decreased considerably.

Perhaps those weekly salts became a habit, or perhaps my aunt really convinced me that salts helped, for just the other day I looked at my ankles, and seeing them swollen I thought to myself, "My kidneys need flushing." I went straight to the store and bought a package of epsom salts. Carefully I measured my two heaping teaspoonfuls and stirred them into a glass of water. I swallowed them with gusto, and back again came that old, nauseated feeling. Back again, too, came my aunt's argument for the value of salts, so I lay still as a corpse and managed to keep them down, but oh, what a feeling.

You may like mineral oil, castor oil, Ex-lax, Milk of Magnesia, or Lawrence Welk's Serutan, but as for me, when there's a house-cleaning job to be done, just give me good old epsom salts!

Here are some miscellaneous remedies I gathered:

Wild catnip was dried in the summer and steeped into a tea for babies with colic.

Yarrow was dried and the tea used for yellow jaundice and liver trouble.

Onion syrup was a common cure for colds.

Senna leaves, available at the co-op, were steeped for measles.

For toothache, a swallow's nest was heated in the oven and applied to the aching jaw. My dad once heated a salt sack full of bran in the oven, and I laid my aching jaw on this and finally fell asleep. Any extract containing a little alcohol was also used: a toothpick with a little roll of cotton was dipped in the flavoring and rubbed around the aching tooth.

Warts would theoretically vanish if you stole your mother's dish rag, rubbed it on the wart, and then hid it. Another cure was greasy bacon rinds rubbed over the wart. Uncle Johnny always paid a penny for every wart he saw on a child. Whether the warts left or not, the kid got an all-day sucker out of the deal.

Coal oil was used for croup.

Bean poultices were the remedy for mumps.

Salt water, vermifuge, and squash seeds were considered effective against worms.

Wild grape root, steeped, treated canker. Some made canker cure from alum, copperas, goldenseal, and alcohol.

Nosebleed responded to brown paper under the lip and a knife on the back of the neck.

Peppermint tea cured vomiting.

A sore throat felt better when fat bacon dipped in coal oil was tied around it.

Coal oil was also good for lice.

Sulphur and alcohol treated the itch.

Lard, sulphur, and alcohol were sovereign against impetigo.

Cough medicine consisted of horehound and licorice.

Garden sage in the spring purified the blood.

Arnica weed was made into a salve for sores.

Lard and camphor were used for chapped hands.

Saffron tea was supposed to be good for rash.

In case of pneumonia, a mustard plaster was an old standby, with some preferring "grease plasters" of lard, mustard, pepper, and ginger. The co-op had cans of Denver mud, which also worked for pneumonia.

Ward's liniment was used internally and externally, for both man and beast, for stomach trouble, rheumatism, arthritis, and every ache.

Flaxseed meal in a poultice drew out boils. As a last resort, a beer bottle was filled with steam and placed over the boil. The steam would hold the bottle on until the boil broke and drained. Meanwhile, the sufferer was justified in groaning!

## Our Ward Mother

As the bishop is the father of the ward, so his wife assumes the role of mother. A legendary ward mother was Agnes B. Jardine, the wife of John Jardine, Clarkson's early bishop. She was the ward mother when I was a baby and as I grew up I was often reminded of her virtues.

The Jardines accepted the gospel in Scotland and later came to America. They lived first in Wellsville and faced near starvation. One winter they lived on frozen turnips; another winter, their only food was squash with a little flour for the father who was doing manual labor.

They were then called to go to Clarkston where John was to be the new bishop. Obedient to the Church for which they had sacrificed their all, they moved to Clarkston and built the home now owned by Arville

Buttars.

Agnes was a precise woman with never a stray lock or a grease spot on her clothing. Today we might call her petite and dainty with little feet and pretty hands. She was proud and wore her fingerless gloves and dress bonnet with queenly dignity.

As the wife of the bishop, Agnes helped take care of the tithing and fast offering which was paid in kind. Bishop Jardine managed the co-op store, and it was Agnes's job to order the merchandise and to take eggs and butter to Logan to exchange for needed commodities. The journey began at four o'clock in the morning so she could reach Logan before the butter melted in the wagon box.

It was also her duty to be hostess to all the Church officials and salesmen that came to town. She was a good cook and an immaculate housekeeper. With her friendly personality, her guests were many and their complaints few. She had the gift of hospitality, even in straitened circumstances. Of one Fourth of July, she said, "We had the Archibalds with us for dinner. We had all the pigweed and mustard greens we could eat, besides plenty of bread and milk."

Agnes loved the customs of her native land. She danced the highland fling and read the poetry of Robert Burns.

Agnes stood by her husband in every way, until a call came from the Church leaders that was very hard to bear. Polygamy was being practiced and the pressure upon bishops to accept this principle was great. Agnes had borne her husband nine children; she had stood by him in famine and hardship; and now he had decided to marry a girl younger than her youngest daughter. There were tears and tension in the Jardine home. Agnes felt that she could not share the man she loved, and the bishop was just as determined that he would follow the teaching of his Church. He married his child-wife, as he sincerely believed he should do. When Agnes saw him coming home for the first time after his marriage, she buried her head between two feather beds and sobbed bitterly. As he entered the house, she held his face in her hands and cried out in the anguish of her soul, "Wee Johnnie, you've gone and left your Wee Nannie."

Her husband, sensing her torture, replied, "My God, why was this required of me?"

There was a happy ending for this great sacrifice, however; John had a stroke and Agnes was unable to lift him. The young wife who bore no children became his nurse, and Agnes loved her for her kindness to them both.

The years passed by. John died. The old house was rented and Agnes went to live with her two daughters, Sarah and Agnes, who were the wives of Charles Shumway. Shortly before her death, Agnes said, "Sarah, why don't you speak to him?"

Sarah said, "To whom, Mother?"

The mother replied, "Your father. He's here waiting for me." And Wee Johnnie claimed his Wee Nannie for time and all eternity.

## John Ravsten, Our Bishop

The beloved bishop during my childhood years was John Ravsten, born 17 February 1871 and died 11 January 1947. He served as bishop of the Clarkston Ward for twenty-two years, from 1902 to 1924.

He was born in Logan, Utah, the son of Bengt Mathias Ravsten and Betty Johnson Ravsten. He married Eliza Christensen and they had six children. They lived on our street, and we children grew up together. Sadness came to our street when Eliza died in 1913 in childbirth with her seventh baby. I was thirteen, and a haunting picture of her in her coffin with a tiny baby on her arm has lingered with me through the years, because I could never understand why she was taken. Whatever Bishop Ravsten's personal pain, his testimony of the justice of God was unshaken. He tried to be mother and father to his large family until he found a new mother for his children: Bertha Nish, one of our school teachers. When he proposed to his second wife, there was much gossiping and the usual comment that he should let his wife "get cold" before he found another. One day as a group of men were discussing this in front of the post office, Jack Thompson said, "You know, men, I got so upset over bishop's getting married again, I knelt down by my old gooseberry bush and prayed about it. And do you know what the Lord said to me? Why he said, 'Jack Thompson, that's none of your business.'"

There were no more comments, and everyone wished the bishop well. We children were particularly happy, for the new mother was full of fun, and a friend to us all. But she died nine years later, leaving behind five more children. Bishop Ravsten had the full responsibility of rearing eleven children in addition to his callings in the ward. He was a kind and loving father. His home was a friendly one and everyone was welcome to come anytime.

Thanks to his granddaughter, Diane Ravsten Griffiths, I have learned even more about his life. He was a great spiritual leader, he loved the people he served, and he, with the guidance of his Father in Heaven in whom he trusted and whom he sought in earnest prayer continually, accomplished much good.

While serving as bishop, he oversaw the construction of a new tithing granary with new scales for weighing tithing wheat and produce. A part of this granary still stands. This was during an era when bishops would spend days at a time receiving tithing wheat or other offering in kind, then hauling the produce by wagon or sleigh to market by horses during the long cold days of winter, leaving before dawn and coming home after dark. From 1910-13, he also oversaw the construction of a beautiful new chapel with a large balcony. Stake conferences were sometimes held there. The building is still standing and used by the Clarkston Ward.

He was bishop during World War I. Despite the patriotism of Clarkston's citizens, the departure of its young men caused much sorrow and anxiety. Bishop Ravsten visited the homes of the servicemen, giving comfort and holding prayers. Now when members of his family sing "How Firm a Foundation," they still think of his life and the faith he transmitted to his descendants. Despite his many trials, that faith was never tested as sorely as in 1944, when he received word of the death of his son, Vance, who was serving his country in Italy—the only one of Clarkston's sixty-one servicemen serving during Word War I who did not return to our ward.

Bishop Ravsten was also active in civic affairs. He was instrumental in the construction of the school house, worked to see it include ninth and tenth grades, and urged young people to get as much education as they could. He was president of the Cache County School Board for many years and was also president of the Clarkston Town Board. He spent many hours straightening out the cemetery records and locating the graves of early settlers. When Church leaders in Logan decided to move Martin Harris's grave from Clarkston to Logan, Bishop Ravsten wrote to President Heber J. Grant for advice. The whole First Presidency came to Clarkston, held a meeting, and later wrote him their agreement with his feelings that the grave should remain in Clarkston. The Church erected a monument to this Book of Mormon witness near his grave in Clarkston. Now an annual pageant honors Martin Harris's achievements and brings visitors from all around the world to the little town of Clarkston.

Perhaps Bishop Ravsten felt strongly about Martin Harris's grave because Martin Harris lived the last years of his life in Clarkston and died there. In fact, no history of Clarkston would be complete without including the written words of three men, Thomas Godfrey, John E. Godfrey, and Alma L. Jensen who saw Martin Harris and heard him give this testimony:

> On July 4, 1875, three of us went to Brother Carbine's home where Martin Harris was staying. He was lying on his bed with his face to the wall. Brother Thomas Godfrey said, "I have brought these young men to see you and ask you if you believe the Book of Mormon to be true."
>
> Brother Harris turned immediately and faced us and said, "No, I don't believe it is true, I know it is true. With these eyes I saw the angel turn the leaves of the golden plates. With these ears I heard the angel say, 'This is a correct record of the people who dwelt upon this continent.'"
>
> We were all thrilled with Brother Harris's earnest, honest testimony.

At the time of Bishop Ravsten's death, he was patriarch of the Smithfield Stake. He was very active in temple and genealogical work.

The greatest desire of his life was to be a good father. He was, according to his children, an extraordinary father, being both mother and father to eleven while serving as bishop. He always considered his children his greatest blessing and deeply appreciated the sacrifices they made so that he could fulfill his many assignments. He greatly prized his membership in the Church and desired sincerely to serve his Heavenly Father to the best of his ability.

# Section III

# Autumn

*Autumn brought other treasures—the tawny topaz of our wheat, the gold of our aspens.*

# Autumn

When the autumn leaves could be piled high into golden mounds, it was time to call the neighbor children around. We threw the potatoes into the leaves and set fire to the whole thing. We danced and yelled and poked the flames of our bonfire. As the flames died down, we singed our eyebrows and burned our fingers trying to roll our potatoes out with a stick. Half done? Skins black with soot? We just sprinkled on salt and lavished on the butter. Delicious!

Saturated with the smell of smoke, eyes smarting from the fumes, we sat around the fire and told ghost stories. What was that strange being that had jumped off Uncle Isaiah's porch three nights in succession? Some thought it was a man, and others swore it wore a bonnet. One of the boys thought it might be an evil spirit. We decided it would be better to go home and we crawled into our straw tick beds shivering. Our fears evaporated with the warmth.

## Mother's Cellar

I wonder what my grandmother or my mother would have thought of a refrigerator or a home freezer? Mother's cooling system was a dirt cellar. Dad dug a hole about ten by ten in the ground and rocked up the sides. Wooden steps covered with a trap door led down into it. He threw dirt on the plank roof, and Mother Nature soon supplied the June grass and marshmallow weeds. Dad was proud of his job, and Mother was serenely happy with this little addition to our home.

I don't know what was so enticing about that dirt roof,

but we always liked to play on it. As sure as we did, black dirt showered on all the contents below. The milk, especially, suffered. Then we were solemnly warned of dire consequences if we played there again—so we stayed away for awhile.

Down in this cellar was a cupboard with screen wire doors to keep out the mice. Even so, we occasionally found a saturated, sleek, gray form floating on a jar of cream. We kept the milk, which was always sour by night, in tin pans on the shelves. Each morning, Mother skimmed the cream into the little brown jar to await churning day, and the "blue John" was poured into the swill bucket for the pigs.

In the left corner of the cellar was a bin where we stored Ben Davis apples in the fall. These apples were so hard we couldn't eat them until spring; but by then, they had acquired a moldy, earthy taste that was anything but appetizing. We wasted nothing in our family, so Mother camouflaged the taste with a little cinnamon and nutmeg, and we enjoyed delicious apple pies. The yellow, upright churn sat beside the apple bin where the dampness of the earth floor kept its wooden staves swollen and tight. The Western washer also needed this damp spot to keep its wooden tub together. There was a shelf for empty fruit bottles, and another shelf for bottled peaches and blue plums. We also boasted a large, wooden meat barrel where five or six pigs were dry-salted every year and the slimy, moldy ends were cut off weekly for the neighbors dogs and cats. With a sack of carrots and a few onions, we were ready for winter. Fortunate was the family who had such a well-filled cellar.

I was startled when I went away to college in Logan and saw head lettuce for the first time. I thought it was a new kind of cabbage. I was amazed to see oranges and bananas in the grocery stores every day. I tasted grapefruit for the first time and learned the difference between sausage and hamburger.

We ate vegetables in the season thereof. What couldn't be dried had to spoil or be given away, and our mouths watered until the next season. Every time I eat string beans in the winter, I think of how I used to long for them as a child when they were a yearly treat.

The first attempt at canning vegetables in Clarkston was a failure. A demonstrator who visited town in 1925 taught the women how to can corn. Several women tried the new method. Later on Sister Shumway opened one of her bottles and, thinking it didn't smell quite right, fed it to her chickens. Horrors! The next morning, they were all dead. The news spread fast. Men dug holes, and by night all of Clarkston's corn, bottles and all, was safely buried beneath the sod. Women threw away their pickled beets, and the skeptical ones continued to boil their jam to that rich, bitter, brown stage.

## Our Two-Room School

The cows have taken over our old rock school house. Stalls replace the benches, and piles of manure bulge out of the windows I used to sit in. But bits of blue calcimined plaster cling to the walls here and there. Memories of my days at school stick just as firmly.

The school had two rooms, a small one for the three beginning grades and a larger one for the advanced students. A small cloakroom, painted a dull, dark green, separated the two classrooms. A water bucket with a long-handled dipper sat on a bench in each room. We would scoop the dipper full, drink to our satisfaction, and pour any surplus back into the bucket. We had occasional outbreaks of typhoid, but no one ever thought to blame this faithful, old bucket. Two nails over the door held switches for the day's discipline. Each teacher's desk held a dunce cap and a long ruler.

Any student who reached the eighth grade felt educated. Some who were brave enough to take a long series of examinations at Logan, and who passed them, were graduated and belonged to an alumni association. That feat received highest recognition in our town and was an honor to be coveted.

In the dusty yard, we played ball. Under the big poplar trees, we played house. The older girls who wore their first stays, or corsets with steel strips, were the mothers. We younger girls willingly accepted their authority, knowing our turn would come in a few years. We brought bits of broken dishes or cane from home for mud pies and continued to learn domesticity.

I think of the frosty mornings when those who sat by the big pot-bellied stove had flushed faces, while those in the corners shivered in their coats. Miss Nish, and later Miss Griffiths, our teachers, made big bottles of flour paste. Every day we cut and pasted blue and yellow chains until we had enough to make a canopy over the drab ceiling. Each day the paste got dry and let a few chains down on our heads, and each day we made more paste and put them back. What a fire hazard it must have been when the old stove gave its morning belch, but luckily the chains never caught fire.

Retentions were common and villainous bullies, who dared talk back to the teacher, were the leaders in the upper grades. When these self-appointed leaders wanted a day off from school, they arrived early in the morning and stuffed the stovepipe full of rags. When the fire was started, the smoke immediately poured forth, the trustees were summoned, and school was dismissed for the day. The trustees would clean out the rags and threaten to expel the next boy who dared do such a trick, but they never found the culprits and we enjoyed our unexpected holidays.

Uncle Billy Clark, one of the trustees, delighted in coming to school. In the fall, he arrived carrying a brown, straw basket on his arm which contained the year's supply of notebooks and paper. Uncle Billy always hummed briskly and his feet kept time to the tune. First we heard tumptedy—dum-dum, and then in walked Uncle Billy all smiles.

My Grandpa Barson, another trustee, enjoyed periodic visits at the school. The students gathered around him as he asked such questions as: "Who is president of the United States?" "How many here are Democrats?" Those who were lucky in answering received pennies or nickels that he fished from down deep in his purse. That purse made him an ever-popular visitor.

Among our semi-annual visitors were Superintendent R. V. Larsen and Miss Peterson, the music teacher. Superintendent Larsen supplied just enough masculine dignity to keep order for Miss Peterson when she taught us to sing. I paid more attention to Miss Peterson herself than to her instruction. She had a mass of yellow hair that she wore in a big, braided bob at the back. Her black satin dress always made me want to run my hands over its smooth, shiny surface. As she walked down the aisle, the fragrant smell of bergamot accompanied her.

She would take the tuning fork and tap it on the desk before she pitched each song. We liked to hear her sing, but there's something that makes school kids always want to test the mettle of a stranger. When the grins and titters became too numerous, a stern look from R.V. Larsen put us in place. As I watch the maples turn red and yellow in the fall, I always sing the song Miss Peterson taught us:

> There's a purple tint on the woodland leaves,
> And the winds are up all day.
> There's a rustling heard in the yellow sheaves,
> And it seems to sadly say

64

Sweet summer, sweet summer,
Sweet summer's gone away.
Sweet summer, sweet summer,
Sweet summer's gone away.

School pranks were rampant. Miss Nish could not sing, and someone had the bright idea to request "The Star-Spangled Banner" for our opening song. We had all been warned to stop when we came to the high notes and let Miss Nish take them alone. The appointed morning arrived, and we began our national anthem with more vim and volume than ever before. As we reached "And the rocket's red glare" there was a sudden death-like silence and Miss Nish, with a lone off-tune crescendo, dangled alone. The students roared with laughter. She was embarrassed but showed no signs of anger. She was the good sport then that we always found her to be.

The boys took delight in putting leafy branches under the seats in the girls' outside privy. The privies' outside enclosure made the interiors dark, and any girl who sat down on the leaves came up with a ticklish yell. The boys were not too far distant to enjoy the screams of recognized voices. These privies were whitewashed annually, covering the yearly record of vulgarity and who loved whom.

Peanut showers were annual festivals. Some of the older girls took up a collection from the students and bought the teacher a dish, side combs, or hankies from the co-op store, and spent the rest for peanuts. Some who held a grudge against the teacher brought their own sack of peanuts with a few "nigger toes," as we called Brazil nuts, mixed in. With a sure eye and a straight aim, they tried to even the score.

Corporal punishment was almost a daily affair. When one of the big boys called Mr. Hoskins, one of our teachers, a "dirty b—," Mr. Hoskins grabbed him from his seat by the hair of his head and shook him soundly. He shoved him back with a thud. The boy looked up at him coolly and addressed him again with the same appellation. The teacher was in a dilemma. He hated to punish the boy again, but to save face he could not be called such names. A death-like silence spread over the room as beating number two began. He jerked the boy up by the collar and hit him on the back with doubled up fists, telling him with each blow that he would not be called those names. Some of the smaller girls began to cry, and all of us were jerking nervously in our double seats. The teacher put the boy back in his desk with another crash. The boy, who was used to such experiences at home, looked up at him without shedding a tear and repeated his chosen terminology.

This time the exhausted pedagogue pointed to the door and yelled, "Get out of here."

The boy sauntered to the door, paused in the entrance, looked back stubbornly, and repeated, "You dirty b—."

The teacher slumped in his chair. He wiped his brow with trembling hands as he tried to regain his composure. He handed me *Ben Logan* by Horatio Alger and said, "Read this." Surprised and with my heart still pounding, I fumbled and stammered. I had to ask him how to pronounce words I already knew. The recess bell finally rang, and we filed out, happy to get a breath of fresh air and to be out of the tension. The boy was back to school the next morning. That was another day.

Most of the students walked to school and went home for lunch with no regard for the deep snow or cold weather. Some rode their ponies to school. Some parents delivered their children in a buggy or a sleigh as the season demanded.

Seasons have come and gone, and the boys and girls who attended that old school have gone with them. As I visit my hometown, I pause to look at my school, just "a ragged beggar sunning."

## When I Become a Teacher

For a large share of my adult life, I was a teacher myself. And things look a little different from the other side of the desk. . . .

English was a headache one day with a bunch of kids who didn't care about learning. One boy grumbled, "I don't care who wrote what. What difference will that make in my life?" A group of farm workers were sauntering down the road toward the beet field and I gestured at them, "Look, that's the way *they* feel." He continued to look blank and bored.

As the day ended, a student stopped me in the hall and handed me a copy of *The Scroll,* our school paper. The first thing that hit my eye was "Marching Corp News." I gritted my teeth. I had had the word *corps* written in four-inch letters on my chalkboard all week.

In my wrath, I thought of a teacher I remembered as a hot-headed, undignified man. When we couldn't get our math one day, he held his head and yelled desperately, "Oh, you damned blockheads!" Walking down the hall, right then and there, I forgave him.

Just then, John, one of my students, came up to me with an adoring look in his eyes. "Is there anything I can do to help you?" he asked politely. I looked at him with admiration for the nobility I saw within. John would never know transitive from intransitive verbs, but he would be an honest, upright citizen. I silently radioed him a message, "I love you for what you are, John."

He received the message and radioed back, "I love you, too." Then he watered the flowers in my classroom. Such days are a payoff and an antidote for the bad ones.

A teacher gets to know her students by the themes they

write. One girl wrote how she hated her grandmother. A boy told how the smell of garlic on a teacher's breath nauseated him. But one boy's story of his pony won an "A" for originality. He told how his pony bucked him off, balked at critical times, and often ran home and left him to walk. He ended his theme by saying, "I don't know whether there is a resurrection for horses or not, but if there is, and I see that pony again, I'll walk up and say, 'Hello, you little brown son-of-a-b—.'"

Whenever a student sluffs, I think of Lora. The temptation of a green, warm April day was too much for her and her friends. They made their getaway from an outside P.E. class and thumbed a ride to Preston. As they strolled down Main Street, the first person they met was Lora's dad.

"What are you doing in town this time of day?" he asked.

"I had a toothache, and I got the girls to come with me," Lora replied innocently. "I'm going to see Dr. Evans."

The father scanned the girls' solemn faces and replied, "I'll go with you. I'm in no hurry."

"Which tooth is aching?" the dentist asked, and Lora pointed it out. "I don't believe it is worth filling," he said gravely.

"Go ahead and pull it then," Lora's dad said. "There's no use of the girl missing school again on account of a toothache."

And the dentist pulled the tooth!

As a teacher, I might have sided with the dad on that experience; but I was with my kids when it came to Mrs. Kelley. Poor Mrs. Kelley was a misfit in our country school in Dayton, Idaho. She had been hired in a last-minute emergency and was bored from the time she saw the school. She hated country life and openly declared that she didn't know what she had done to end up in such a forsaken place. The students felt it was their loyal duty to retaliate. And so the clash intensified each day. One day the boys decided to make her angry; and while she was at the height of her fury, Del was to take her picture. Accordingly, Roger and Jerry started a little fist fight. The commotion was not quite loud enough, so two boys climbed up on their desks. That did it. With a volley of adjectives not becoming a teacher, she descended on them. Del carefully focused his camera at the climax of her wrath. Flash! Snap! went the camera amid a roar of laughter. With their intentions accomplished, the boys settled down and behaved.

About a week later, the heartless wretches brought the photograph to class.

"Look, Mrs. Kelley," they laughed.

"Oh, my G—," she cried as she looked at it. "If I ever had to drive by this place again, I'd detour!"

## General Merchandise

Our town had two general stores. One was the co-op, which has been remodeled into a modern grocery store, and the other was owned by the Larsen sisters. The co-op sold stock and paid a small yearly dividend on the money invested. It was approved by the Church, and consequently, the most devout were supposed to do their buying there.

Both stores were expected to carry everything a family needed: food, clothing, dishes, dry goods, hardware, toys, jewelry, and medicine. For small purchases, the usual legal tender was a basket of eggs. On the return trip the basket might contain a pair of long, black stockings, a hair ribbon, a pound of cheese, a few nails, and a mousetrap. The shopper nearly always carried, in the other hand, a gallon can of coal oil.

Clarkston conventions allowed shoppers to go from one store to the other if one lacked a needed item. Shoppers also felt free to point out to the clerks any variation in prices between the two. Uncle Tom, the manager of the co-op, sat on a high stool at a high desk just inside the door to the left. He had accidentally discharged a gun into his foot, as a young man, and was crippled thereafter, so he stuck pretty close to his perch. He often jokingly said, "If I hadn't been crippled in the head, I wouldn't be crippled in my foot."

Uncle Tom was usually looking over his charge accounts, with some doubt and wonder, because people paid their bills at the wheat harvest. If it was poor, due to frost, hail, or drought, Uncle Tom was left holding the bag. If bad luck dogged a farmer the second year, Uncle Tom still seldom refused credit, and I imagine several long-unpaid bills could be found upon his books to this day.

Kids who were fortunate enough to find a new nest of eggs got one to exchange for candy; and as they entered the store, Uncle Tom in a sing-song voice would lament, "Um, um, sugar's gone 'hup.' Not much candy for a penny." We kids wondered at that ever-increasing price of sugar.

Close to the front of the store was a glass case containing side combs with shiny sets, bone hair pins, breast pins with big blue stones, a few rings fitted into a red, plush case, hat pins, knitting needles with fancy knobs, and crochet hooks in three sizes that folded and fit into a designed tin handle, beads, and bone-handled pocket knives.

On the left were kegs of pickles sold by the quart, rings of bologna swimming in salty brine; containers of cinnamon, nutmeg, tumeric, and mustard; a large round cheese covered with cheesecloth with the cracked, dry edge showing through, and a shiny cleaver attached to the case.

In the back of the store stood rows of boxes of buttoned shoes, long-handled underwear, corsets so heavy with steel that they seemed more like body casts than girdles, a tall glass case on the counter for ribbon of assorted widths, colors, and patterns, and various sizes of black stockings.

At the right were wedding presents: dishes, tubs, buckets, dishpans, brooms, washboards, and towels; fluffy canton flannel for baby diapers, linen for graduation dresses or burial; calico, and a few pieces of Sunday dress goods. You knew you'd meet someone in the same print, but the dress would be made differently so you still kept your individuality.

Aunt Ruth, Uncle Tom's second wife, was a seasoned, efficient helper. She knew where everything was and what its price was without looking. She could cut a pound of cheese within a fraction of an ounce and estimate a yard of calico to one-fourth of an inch. Aunt Ruth radiated confidence in buying to the customer, visiting with them as she worked: "How is Mama? How is the baby? I heard there was whooping cough in town." Any bit of news was passed on to all who entered the store.

This was no serve-yourself store. Aunt Ruth's legs did all the running while you sat on a stool and waited. If you looked longingly through the glass showcase at trays of sour drops, horehound, and taffy, Aunt Ruth just slipped a piece in your mouth. She always gave full measure or a little more.

Fresh vegetables in a store were unknown; but on the Fourth of July and Christmas, Uncle Tom and Aunt Ruth stocked extravagant luxuries: bananas, oranges, sometimes lemons, and a big bag of peanuts.

The co-op contained the only telephone in town, and few knew how to use it. Aunt Ruth called the doctor if someone needed some stitches and phoned in orders for white velvet and casket handles to ZCMI. Visiting over the telephone was unthinkable.

Shoplifting was uncommon; but if a clerk left the strap off the back door during noon hour, adventuresome school boys entered and raided the candy. That afternoon, peppermints, gumdrops, and chewing gum passed from dirty overall pockets to every scholar who refused to tell on the giver. We were not bothered with professional thugs. They could not find their way in and out of our little town without being observed the whole way, and they took no chances.

Lettie and Mary Larsen owned and managed the other general store. Both were prim old maids who attended strictly to their own business. Lettie was tall with sallow skin and a dark bob on top of her head. Her dresses, or waists, always had a high neckline with a ruffle of embroidery or a black ribbon tight around her neck. Her fingers were long and bony but efficient at wrapping parcels and breaking twine. Some say that Lettie could play the organ, but few ever heard her.

Mary was shorter and more cordial, although she shared much of her sister's tenacious reserve. Mary wore black dresses most of the time with fancy leg-of-mutton sleeves. She was said to be an expert seamstress, but neither sister asked questions or volunteered information. Conversation was limited to the weather, and everyone accepted at face value the sign in the candy case, "Positively no loafing here."

The Larsen sisters also ran their charge accounts; and like the co-op, took their losses on bad debts with stoicism. It was considered quite improper to mail out a statement of debts. A storekeeper was lacking in stamina if he didn't ask in person for payment. If the debtor could not pay his bill but still had money to go to Logan, that was his business. But as a whole, people thought highly of a good name and a clear conscience and paid the stores as they sold their wheat.

72

Mary and Lettie took little part in religious activities except for donating to every worthy cause. Some said they made money on their store, but that was a matter of speculation.

## A Halloween Party

Grandpa "Sanko" recorded this account of a Halloween party on 7 November 1908:

> On Saturday evening the spooks visited the home of Mr. and Mrs. P.S. Barson. Twenty of them, dressed in white and disguised, took possession of the parlor. They were a dumb lot, no words being spoken for fear of disclosing identities. The string band that accompanied them played a march and the fun began. All present were required to guess the identity of each spook after which they unmasked. There was great rejoicing when old friends met and unmasked. They played games and sang songs until midnight when the big Halloween cake was cut, each portion containing some little gift, such as rings, thimbles, charms, and beads to tell the destiny of the one drawing them.

## Calf Ghosts

The Halloweeners were out after dark, looking for mischief—and found it. Aunt Tildy had left her washing on the line, and Uncle Jack's calves were close by. The combination was irresistible, and they quickly pulled the white long-handled underwear off the line and dressed the calves. The "ghosts" wandered through town stopping here and there to eat on a front lawn. Even the kids that dressed up the calves got a little frightened. From a distance they really looked ghostly. This was *too* realistic. The kids scampered home.

# Uncle Jack, Master of Splints

Everybody in our town loved Uncle Jack and respected him for his healing arts. Whenever he drove the cows to the pasture, after Aunt Hanner had milked them, kids on either side of the street came out to talk to him. He would tease the boys about some homely little girl and the girls about some boy, then would go laughing down the street to the cow pasture, leaving the secretly pleased youngsters sputtering protests.

He always carried a big stick. I never saw him strike a cow or dog, and he didn't need a cane, but the stick was his constant companion.

One day my mother was scrubbing the floor and accidentally shoved a large sliver far underneath her fingernail. She tried a needle, tweezers, and pliers, but the sliver would not move. After a half hour of hopeless trying, we knew this was a case for Uncle Jack. One of my brothers went to get him, and Uncle Jack, with his genial manner, was soon on the scene.

Uncle Jack had probably never heard of psychology, but he practiced it quite unconsciously. He looked around and saw that we children were all tense and nervous. We didn't want our mama hurt. He began to laugh and twist the ends of his white mustache. We knew that something funny was coming as he asked, "Did you hear about my ol' lady under the table?" We began to relax as he told the story of Aunt Hanner and the visitor.

"The other day," he began, "My ol' lady saw a woman that she was mad at coming up our path. She began to jaw like women do and said she wouldn't let the ol' so-and-so in. So I sez, 'Hanner, I'll tell you what to do. You just crawl under the table and I'll tell her you're not home.'"

"She thought that was a good idea and quietly crawled under and pulled the oil cloth low on one end so she couldn't be seen. You know I like a good joke."

He paused in the story and chuckled. We knew the big climax was coming.

"When I heard that knock on the door, I sez, 'Come in. I guess you want to see the ol' lady. Well, here she is under the table.'"

We were all laughing now. "Hanner, she came out of her hiding place and sez, 'Jack, you ol' devil, I'll fix you for this.'"

Still laughing, he said, "Now, let's get after that sliver." He took out a large pocket knife and opened the biggest blade. "Come, Samanthy Jane," he said to Mother. (Samanthy Jane was a common nick-name, a term of endearment.) "Just turn your head the opposite way." Mother nervously obeyed, he split the nail neatly, she gave a scream, and we all ran to peek at the operation. Uncle Jack probed and punched and in a minute proudly displayed the big sliver on the blade of his knife. He smiled as we thanked him and he went his way, never knowing or worrying what emergency would come next.

He always kept splints ready for broken bones and straightened many a crooked limb for both men and beasts. One day our colt broke its leg, and of course, we sent immediately for Uncle Jack. He looked the colt over, took a straw and chewed on it, and then made his decision. "If that thing was mine," he said, "I'd hit it in the head."

"Oh, but it's such a pretty colt," we begged. "We couldn't do that."

"Well, I'll set it if you want, but it won't last."

True to his prediction, in three days the colt was dead, and we were sorry we'd let it suffer.

Uncle Jack was not a church-goer. He lived his

religion in a practical way. He asked nothing for his services, he received nothing, and was happy.

## Uncle Joe: Music-maker

What would Clarkston have done without Uncle Joe? We relied on him for every occasion that required music. He led the congregation and the choir in our Sunday meetings. He fiddled for the dances and all the parties, and if a politician needed a musical number for a rally, he sought Uncle Joe. He played for the wedding dance of my Grandpa and Grandma Godfrey, and at their golden wedding, he was still in trim and played for a lively cotillion.

Uncle Joe had no musical training. He was just one of those born with a keen sense of melody and rhythm. A sour note always made him wrinkle his forehead, and rhythm that faltered for a fraction of a count produced an awful scowl. People could tell how the music was going by looking at Uncle Joe better than by relying on their own sense of harmony.

When Uncle Joe played for a dance, no one was ever caught with his foot in the air. That accented down beat helped even the poorest dancers stay in step. He tapped his foot gently as he led his choir, and just one look at him as he lifted his hand-carved willow baton made us want to open our mouths wide and sing, not with squeaky, shallow, nasal tones, but deep, way down deep tones, just like Uncle Joe.

Worldly goods did not bother Uncle Joe. He possessed the "merry heart that doeth good like a medicine." He brought joy as he sang "Alice Ben Bolt" and "When You and I Were Young, Maggie" at parties. He gave religious fervor and inspiration with "Lo, the Mighty God Appearing" and consolation to the bereaved with "Oh, Grave Where Is Thy Victory?" and "Shall We Meet Beyond The River?"

As he grew older, he was the first to congratulate a young musician after a public rendition. One day as I stepped down from the organ almost in tears over the mistakes I had made, there stood Uncle Joe. He put his arm around me and said, "You made that old organ sound fine today."

"Oh, Uncle Joe, didn't you hear those awful mistakes?" I stammered, teetering on the verge of tears.

"But you'll never make the same mistakes again," he consoled me.

Instead of going home and crying, I practiced, just because of Uncle Joe.

## Uncle Tom, Wielder of Forceps

My grandfather, Thomas Godfrey, was known to all our community as "Uncle Tom." When every toothache remedy failed, the poor victim was taken with trembling knees to Uncle Tom for the awful extraction. First, Grandpa would get his silver-rimmed glasses and balance them in the middle of his nose. Next, he removed the dish towel from the victim's swollen jaw and had him sit on a chair by the window. He looked long and hard, adjusting the sufferer's head in the light and exhorting him constantly to "open just a little wider." Sometimes he called Uncle Jim to take a look before he made the fateful decision. With his younger eyes he could confirm the diagnosis.

After assuring the poor kid that he would feel better with that awful thing out, Grandpa went to the cupboard for the forceps. The child would watch him unwrap the newspaper from those shiny forceps, which looked big enough to pull an elk's tooth, and would often make one last jump for freedom, bounding out of the door and into the yard. The parent, catching the runaway, would offer gifts of candy, wipe away the tears, and bring him back. The parent would hold the child, Uncle Jim would pry his mouth open, and Grandpa would begin.

Pulling and twisting with the sweat dripping from his nose, Grandpa would relinquish his hold for a new try at a different angle, and the little victim, seeing a drop of blood on those awful prongs, would scream. About this time, Grandma would go feed the chickens or find some other outdoor errand to get away from the blood-curdling yells.

All redoubled their holds, and once more twist, push, scream—until Grandpa would proudly flourish the offending tooth.

After such an ordeal the awful forceps were rinsed with cold water and wrapped in newspaper until the next desperate victim came along. My dad finally inherited them. I used to look at them and think what tales of misery those forceps could tell.

## Clarkston's Missionaries

Clarkston Ward dutifully heeded the admonition, "Go ye into all the world to preach the gospel," and regularly kept two missionaries in the field. Many felt if they ever refused a call, God would pour out his wrath upon them and responded, even when their circumstances meant that the call would entail real hardship. An exception was one aunt of mine who had no fear of divine or Satanic punishment. When her son was called on a mission to Africa, she tartly told the bishop, "If you want someone to preach to them black buggars, you can go yourself; my boy hain't a-goin'." The boy didn't go and didn't seem to suffer any dire consequences.

A missionary farewell party had a traditional format. It was always held on a week night. The bashful missionary said a few words, and sometimes his father did, too. Then someone more fluent spoke on the privilege of going on a mission and the glory of saving one soul. There was a vocal solo, and then the name of each person who had contributed to the missionary's lean purse was read out, along with the amount. You sat up straight with pride if your contribution was among the highest and slumped or fingered the hymn book if you were down the list.

The program always ended with closing remarks by the bishop and a tearful singing of "God Be with You." The evening concluded with a dance, the home-town orchestra always playing free for such an occasion. Members of the family and the sweetheart, soon to forget her tearful pledges, saw the elder off from Cache Junction.

I liked to hear my Grandfather Godfrey tell stories of his mission. He was serving in the Southern States Mission when Elders Berry and Gibbs were killed. He proudly displayed a picture of B. H. Roberts disguised as a ruffian when he got the bodies of the elders to send home.

Many of our missionaries told both breathtaking and faith-promoting stories while in the South. Several were chased by dogs. One was tied and whipped with a hickory switch. Although this man carried scars to his grave, I have heard him bear testimony that he felt no pain, and his testimony never wavered.

Another told of being given a glass of milk, but his hand shook until he could not get the glass to his mouth. Those in the room were amazed; and he soon learned that the milk was poisoned. This same missionary balanced this faith-promoting one with a far earthier experience: "One day I went into a stable to pray and knelt down on a nice, clean pile of straw. Suddenly, the straw began to move and out scrambled a big pig. The pig gave a grunt and I gave a jump and that ended my praying that day."

Some of our missionaries went to foreign countries and came back to bear testimony in strange tongues. I listened round-eyed to a missionary from Hawaii who told of "poi" made from rotten bananas and served on leaves for plates. The plates and no dishwashing sounded appealing, but raw fish tails and scrambled eggs containing unhatched chicks would test the faith of the most devout. Some of the mothers gagged and wiped their eyes at these accounts.

I remember when John Loosli, the father of three boys was called to the Swiss-German Mission. This was the birthplace of his parents, and he was very happy to go. Just as he received his release, after fulfilling an honorable mission, he took sick and died. When the message was relayed to Clarkston, the whole town mourned and the eternal question of "Why?" was in every heart. Our leader told us that God moves in a mysterious way and mortal man should not question His wisdom; but in our human thinking, it still seemed unjust. The twenty-eight-day wait for the body to arrive seemed endless. All the family's dreams of having their farm in order for a returning father dissolved in grief. Finally, a telegram came saying the body would be in Cache Junction 26 August 1908. The entire population of Clarkston drove down in horse and buggies. To add to our emotions, the train was an hour late. As we nervously waited, we walked the tracks and listened. At last a shrill whistle sounded down the canyon, and in a few minutes, the black monster puffed into view. We clung to our parents as the fearful engine belched its steam, and the loud gongs of the bell sent cold shivers through us. The brakes screeched. There was a bump and a thud on each car, and the train stopped.

Someone with a little blue cap pulled a cart along the track and a big side door on a car opened revealing a heavy, wooden box. An awful stillness spread over the crowd, broken now and then by a low sob, a baby's cry, or a nervous horse cramping the buggy wheels. We watched the big box loaded on the cart and, unashamed of tears, wiped our eyes.

Then a problem developed. The bishop measured the box and then went over to Lindquist's funeral surrey, drawn by a team of white horses—the best that Cache Valley had to offer. But the high German casket would not fit. A white-top buggy was hastily made ready, the casket loaded into it, and the people in their buggies formed in line according to their relation to the deceased. Slowly and sadly we crossed the river and went up the hill back home. A cloud of dust spread over the winding cortege and with it a feeling of mournful satisfaction. At last our elder was home.

The meetinghouse had been decorated with many yards of white bunting caught up in scallops with white satin bows. There were sprays of real carnations with their cloyingly sweet, sad smell and potted geraniums on the organ and the pulpit. All was clean and still as we entered. Dr. Seymour B. Young, one of the Seven Presidents of Seventy, was present. He spoke at the funeral and opened the casket at the graveyard. A few looked at Elder John, but most preferred to remember him as they had last seen him.

His good wife never wavered spiritually, but physically, the shock took its toll and she suffered from years of poor health. Through it all, she raised her sons to be church leaders as their father would have wanted them to be.

Another elder who returned after filling an honorable mission was giving his report in church when he suddenly lost control of himself. His eyes seemed to go around in his head and he was unable to speak. A member of the bishopric said, "He is possessed of an evil spirit. Brother Heggie, go for some consecrated oil and we will rebuke it."

Brother Heggie left immediately and soon returned with the oil. Some of the children heard the words "evil spirit" and, terrified, ran from the building in fear of being seized themselves. A death-like silence spread over the congregation as the young man was laid on the bench. Selected men gathered around him and, by the power of the priesthood, commanded the evil spirit to depart. Meeting was dismissed, and a congregation—half uplifted, half upset—returned home.

## Sausage and a Balloon

I was always torn between two conflicting emotions at hog-killing time. I felt sorry for the animal to be slaughtered, yet I could hardly wait for a plate full of onion sausage. And Dad always blew up the bladder of the deceased pig and made a balloon for us children to play with until it dried up and popped.

The day before the killing, Dad built a platform out of old boards and set it on top of a couple of saw-horses. He "charred" the vinegar barrel by lighting a little smudge in it to take out the smell of vinegar, then invited two strong-armed uncles to assist.

On the morning of the slaughter, Mother placed two boilers full of water over the roaring fire on the kitchen range. As the water heated, steam ran down the wall, leaving black streaks wherever there had been any dust on the white-wash. The men sat around visiting and taking turns sharpening their butcher knives on a whetstone. About every five minutes, someone would take the lid off the boiler to see if the water was hot and out would fly an extra cloud of steam. I dressed quickly and ran down to Grandma Barson's, where I couldn't hear the hog squeal as he got his throat cut.

The men roped the pig, led it out of the pen, and two men threw the pig on its back and held it while the third, who considered himself an expert at finding the jugular vein, would haggle away. The pig's blood-curdling screams could be heard for blocks. After its throat was cut, the pig was allowed to run around with the blood gushing until it collapsed. Then the men lifted it to the platform, poured the scalding water into the barrel, and tilted the barrel just enough so that the hog could be pushed in and out with one man on each hind leg. Swish, splash, went the hog back and forth in the barrel. Then when one of the men could pull the hair off easily, they began scraping the hide until the skin was white and free of bristles.

They then fastened a singletree between its hind legs and hoisted the carcass to a board fastened high between two poles. Dad cut it down the belly and removed the entrails and leaf lard. What a nauseating smell as the liver and heart were removed! I marveled how I could like sausage when I saw what it was made with. The blood and hair were left on the ground for the winter wind and rain to remove, and the neighboring dogs and cats had a midnight feast on the entrails.

By night, the thoroughly chilled form of the hog was carried in and laid on the kitchen table. There Dad sliced out pieces of side pork, ribs, and back bone and rolled them carefully in newspaper. All of us kids carried meat to all our friends and relatives in the neighborhood. The next day I could play with my balloon, and get my hands smelly, greasy, and sticky. In two more days, there would be fresh country sausage seasoned with garden sage and browned onions, as only Mother could cook it.

# Progress Report

"Sanko" wrote this "state of Clarkston" message for the Logan *Journal,* 21 November 1899:

A number of new modern brick residences have been built costing $ 1,500 and $ 2,000. The church has a new roof and they are decorating the inside. A new brick school house has been built costing $ 2,000.

During the thirty-six years that this town has been settled there have been no whiskey shops. Good health, peace and plenty abound. There are no poor in the ward. Only two aged people are given a little help.

# Section IV

# Winter

*Winter brought pearls—a landscape glowing white as far as the eye could see— and, under the bright blue sky, diamonds dazzling in the snow.*

#  Winter

As winter deepened and snow drifts mounted higher than the fences, our neighbors literally dropped in for the evening. No family had more fun with less money than ours. In fact, money could not buy our homemade fun. There were games of "Thimble Spy," guessing initials, and "Who Stole the Bishop's Cow?" In this game, the blindfolded "it" stood in the center, trying to guess who was poking him or her vigorously in the stomach with a broom handle. Honey candy and pans of apples satisfied everyone's taste.

On quiet evenings, by the light of a coal oil lamp, Dad read us Hurlbut's Bible Stories or sawed away on an old fiddle. We sang to his accompaniment with a song in our hearts as well as in our throats.

Suddenly the wind would bang the door, and a flurry of snow would beat against the window. Blizzard! There would be paths to shovel in the morning, and maybe we couldn't get to school, but right now there was corn to pop and butter to melt, and Mother was telling the story of the three men who went out to find the smallest thing in the world. As one man found a dog so small it would fit in a nutshell, the wind rushed through the window casings making the lamp sputter and almost die away. "We'd better nail a quilt over the window," Mother said. "The storm may blow out the lamp." As Dad nailed the quilt on, we put on our coats and piled more fuel into the stove. Mother heated a flat iron for each one to take to the cold bed. There was nothing to fear, though the storm raged without. With our flat irons and at least two brothers or sisters, we could burrow into the little hammock that each body had molded into the straw. That snugness was sweet, indeed.

## Tell Me a True Story

Storytelling was a great favorite on winter nights. Both my mother and my father were good storytellers, and my grandpas' stories were the best of all! What fun to snuggle together by the fire and listen to adventure and tragedy, humor and real-life happenings more interesting than any fairy tale. Many of the stories I heard as a child, I wrote down later in my life. Some were stories about Clarkston (many of which I have already included), some were about pioneers and Indians, and many stories were told about people my grandparents knew or heard about when they were young in the 1800's. Here are some of the stories I remember best:

## Brigham Young's Visit

My Grandfather Godfrey loved to tell the story of Brigham Young's visit to Clarkston on June 4, 1870. When the brethren learned that President Young was coming, they cut willows from along the creek bank and built a shady bowery for his meeting with the discouraged Saints. There had been trouble with the Indians, and the diet of greens, a little bread, and lumpy dick (milk and flour) was neither satisfying nor nourishing.

The great leader arrived, and after hearty handshakes with all, he stepped up on a box and began to address the people. He looked over the vast expanse of sagebrush and then looked down at a distressed people. Raising his cane and pointing all around him, he made this prophetic utterance in clear, articulate tones, "Some of you will live to see the day when all of these barren hills will be waving with golden grain. The desert shall blossom as the rose. There will be food and plenty for all."

The people were satisfied. Their prophet had spoken, and they were filled with new hope as they worked to make that prophecy come true. Homesteaders built crude log cabins on the desolate hills and began to plow. Seed for dry-farming was procured, and before many years had passed, every hill waved with grain.

Lucy Mickelson remembers another Brigham Young story: In 1865 there was considerable trouble with the Indians in Clarkston, and one was killed. At a conference in the fall of 1866 President Brigham Young made a prophecy that the man who killed this Indian should have his right hand wither. Thomas Godfrey saw this come to pass when a man in Mendon, whose right hand withered, admitted the deed.

## Unexpected Bride

Andrea's lips were parched with fever and a dull pain seemed to split her head. Then as the boat rocked, there came that awful nausea. She had been unremittingly seasick ever since she had set sail with a company of the Danish Saints for Zion. Starving, dehydrated, and feverish, she heard the elders slide another body into the sea. Splash! Swish! The waves lapped it up, and it was gone. Would she be next? No one aboard that little ship thought she could live another day. She turned in her bed and fear shone in her glazed eyes.

"Andrea will never live," cried Elder Jones. "She has given her all for the gospel's sake. She has left her family and friends, she is alone, and it is the least we can do to see that someone will marry her and do her temple work." He looked the crowd over and then made this strange request, "Who will volunteer to marry Andrea and, when we reach the valleys of the mountains, be sealed to her for time and all eternity?"

Thomas Nielson, a fine-looking young Dane stepped forward and said, "I will marry Andrea. You may perform the ceremony right now."

Margrethe, his betrothed, burst into tears, but Elder Jones, looking at him with admiration, hastily performed the ceremony, with Andrea weakly whispering, "I do," while Thomas pronounced the words distinctly. Thomas thought to himself, "This will show Margrethe I'll make the decisions. She's been getting just too bossy of late. This poor girl will be dead in two hours and rolled into the sea. Dead women at the bottom of the ocean can't cause jealousy, then I'll marry Margrethe and perhaps she will have learned a valuable lesson that pouting won't go with me." He went to his cabin quite pleased with himself and his disciplinary tactics.

But Andrea did not die. She clung to life for another week. The following week, she sat up in bed while the sisters braided her dark hair. She was pale and thin and dark circles outlined her eyes, but they gleamed with spunk and determination. Gradually the realization struck her that she was married to a man she scarcely knew, a man who loved another. Thomas never came near her, but as she grew stronger and moved about, she could see him and Margrethe walking hand and hand on the deck, and sometimes she saw him kiss her. The elders felt that Thomas should claim his bride, but Andrea would not agree. Although she felt drawn to the strong young Dane, to take advantage of his act of compassion for her in her death hour was too much for her proud, independent soul. She didn't know how, but she had faith that the Lord would provide a way for her to get out of this dilemma.

The long voyage came to an end, and the little Danish

company found themselves ready to start the trek west. There were a few teams and wagons for the sick and the aged, but most of the company walked. Day after day, Andrea walked behind her sturdy blond husband who walked hand in hand with Margrethe, solicitous of her every whim. Margrethe always cast ugly glances at Andrea, but Andrea never responded in kind.

At night Andrea rubbed buffalo grease on the blistered feet of little Anna and Carl Johnson and told them Hans Christian Andersen's stories from their native land. The children always demanded the tale of how the ugly duckling turned into a beautiful swan. Somehow, Andrea liked that story too. Then when the children were asleep, she heated water over the campfire and bathed Brother Hansen's swollen feet. Other people always came first with Andrea. She had no time for self-pity.

One night she sat late by the campfire making a pair of moccasins for Brother Sorenson whose shoes were worn out. Thomas sat on the other side of the fire mending a broken wheel. "He's big and fine," thought Andrea, "and he is my husband, but I mustn't love him because he loves Margrethe."

Sitting by the fire, Thomas thought, "Andrea is a wonderful woman, so kind, so good, and she is my wife; but she never looks my way."

Each day was much the same. Buffalo chips to gather, scanty meals over a campfire, broken wagons, sickness, and often death. But they pressed forward, ever forward, with legs scratched by sage brush and feet blistered by the hot slick grass. The rough outline of the jagged Rocky Mountains appeared, giving them fresh hope and courage. They knew they would soon reach a new home where they could rest. As they looked with awe at the bold, glaring mountains, a brown doe sauntered out and stared at them curiously. There was the quick crack of a rifle, promising fresh meat for supper.

It was the skilled hands of Andrea who cooked the venison over the campfire, and it was she who saw that all were fed before she ate. Then she retired behind a wagon as the others sang and danced the twilight away, but as the evening prayer was said, she joined the circle and bowed her head in gratitude with the rest. The moon came up and filled the plains with cold, blue light, and a sharp-scented mountain breeze filled the air. Then as they spread out their dirty, worn blankets for the night, Elder Jones sang in his lilting tenor, "And soon we'll have this tale to tell. All is well, all is well."

Day after day, the party moved westward. The trail was littered with cast-off furniture, and always there were graves marked by buffalo skulls and wagon wheels. Then they came to a deep stream. Margrethe sat on the bank and pouted as she waited for Thomas to carry her. Andrea watched out of the corner of her eye as she herself picked up little Anna to help her across the water. She saw Thomas put Margrethe down on the opposite bank with a hard thud, then turn to help others. Andrea smiled to herself as she stepped unhesitatingly into the swirling water.

It was mid-August as the weary company made camp for the last time in Emigration Canyon. The chokecherries were hanging thick on the bushes, and young and old soon had stained, puckered mouths from the first taste of fruit in weeks. There was a spirit of gaiety as they looked down into the valley, and past troubles were forgotten. They could see the faint flicker of the coal oil lamps like tiny fireflies, and the light in their souls glowed, for tomorrow they would see a prophet of God. Andrea looked at the panorama before her. The moon glowed on the great salt sea, and she bowed her head in thanks that she had been permitted to come to this new land.

Suddenly someone stood beside her. He reached for her hand, but she jerked it away. "Andrea," Thomas said, "are you afraid of the new life which lies before you?"

"Afraid? No," she answered warmly. "God has restored my health, and above all he has given me a testimony of the gospel. I have made my way alone and . . ." But she did not finish the sentence and turned quickly away.

As Thomas looked after her, he caught Margrethe staring at the little scene. She laughed mockingly, but for the first time, he did not go to her. He sat down quietly and stared into the valley thinking, seriously thinking.

The next morning was full of excitement as the company descended into the valley. Brethren on horseback met them and led them to the public square where many relatives waited to welcome them. Uncle Hans was there to take Margrethe and her parents to his own comfortable home until they could become established. Thomas avoided Margrethe until, pouting sullenly, she reluctantly climbed into the wagon and drove away.

Brother Peterson called out, "Captain, I have room for another one in my home."

The captain said, "Thomas, you may go with Brother Peterson."

Thomas hesitated, then asked awkwardly, "Brother Peterson, would you have room for my wife, too?"

Andrea stared at him incredulously. A warm flush mantled her cheeks. The captain cleared his throat. Brother Hansen dropped the bucket of water he was carrying and Sister Hansen dabbed at her eyes with her waist apron. Thomas walked over to Andrea and took her by the hand. "Will you come?" he asked tenderly. Andrea could feel strength and security in his touch, but hesitated. The old independence welled up strong in her. She would accept no man's pity. But as she looked up at him, what she saw plainly written on his kind, honest face was love.

"Sure, we can make room for your wife," Brother Peterson answered. "A man should not be without his wife."

And with just a slight quaver in her voice, Andrea squared her shoulders and replied, "Yes, Brother Peterson, we will come."

## A Toll of Six

As you travel along the highway in Franklin County, Idaho, stop at the bridge on the West Cache Canal. There on a sagebrush hill above you, you will see an abandoned cemetery. A few crude headstones stand out among the bunch grass and wild sunflowers, marking the grave of some of the noble men, women, and children who settled in the valley along Bear River.

George Mendenhall and Celeste Ann Mendenhall were among the hardy pioneers of 1852 along the river bottoms, then known as Franklin Meadows. They built a log house at the foot of the little hill, had a family of six, and were happy among relatives and friends. They lived a typical frontier life plowing, reaping, spinning, and trusting in the Lord's protective care. There was no need for a sheriff or lawyer. A man's word was his bond, and if a neighbor needed help, it was freely given with no thought of getting something in return.

The winter months passed by, and then during the end of March, diphtheria broke out and the Mendenhalls were stricken.

"George," called a neighbor from a safe distance outside the house. George appeared at the door, and the neighbor continued, "How many are down with diphtheria today?"

George answered in a melancholy tone, "Two of my children are very sick. We were up all night with Valerie, and now Leslie has taken a turn for the worse."

"Is there anything we can bring you?" called the neighbor.

"Yes, the wood is getting low, burning fires night and day, and we will need a gallon of kerosene before night."

The neighbor, backing away a step each time she spoke, called, "I'll bring it."

In late afternoon, a sister put a package of food over the fence and was almost out of hearing distance before she dared call the family.

"Valerie and Leslie are worse," George called back as he took the bread and dried apples into the house.

The word spread to Dayton, a little town three miles west, that the Mendenhall children were dying. This was more than the kind heart of Aunt Sarah Phillips could stand. Aunt Sarah was a widow with a large family, but she was blessed with a divine touch of healing and never refused to help anyone who needed her. "Lizzie," she said to her daughter, "the Mendenhall children are dying. I feel I must go there. I know the Lord will spare me from the disease and from bringing it home to my children. Will you take care of things while I am gone?"

"Yes, Mother," replied the faithful Lizzie. "And I'll pray for you and the Mendenhalls."

Aunt Sarah alighted from a wagon in front of the Mendenhall home and was greeted with tears of joy and relief. She tied on her white waist apron and set to work, swabbing the swollen throats with drops of turpentine and trying to get the two little ones to swallow oil and sugar. Dark-haired Leslie, just five years old, grew limper and bluer each hour. What could they do? After a final choking spell, he lay lifeless in his mother's arms. There was no time for tears. They turned to Valerie and worked tirelessly, but it was no use. In a few hours, seven-year-old Valerie had also passed away.

Aunt Sarah bathed the little bodies and laid them on

some rough boards beside an open window. Someone brought a sack of snow which they packed in bottles and put around the bodies to keep them cool until burial.

When neighbor Cal Boyce heard of the double tragedy he said, "It hain't right for a father to have to nail a coffin lid on his own children. I am going in and help them."

The willow trees along the river were budding, and the hills were growing freshly bright with June grass, but there was no spring for the Mendenhalls. Three-year-old Leroy fell a victim to the disease. Friends again brought wood, kerosene, and food. They tried to cheer George and Celeste Ann: "Surely God would not ask more of you." But on 27 March, Leroy died and was buried beside his brother and sister. Two weeks later, George's wagon rolled slowly up again to the graveyard hill. This time he and Brother Boyce dug a grave for nine-year-old George. This left the Mendenhalls with only Elvira and a babe-in-arms.

Despite this crushing experience, these pioneers had no time for bitterness. There was work to do. Sustained by their religious belief that death is not the end, that we will meet our loved ones again, they were able to go on.

God blessed these faithful parents with other children. Of course, none ever took the place of those they had lost, but there was music and laughter again in the Mendenhall home. Times grew more prosperous. Hunger and want were driven out, but then in 1902, diphtheria struck again. There were doctors now, but two beautiful Mendenhall girls succumbed. Zella was taken first, and in six more days Elsie followed her. Diphtheria had taken a toll of six from the Mendenhall family.

I stood on the hill and looked at the graves of George and Celeste Ann Mendenhall and their children. A feeling of reverence overwhelmed me as I thought of their courage and stamina. I felt proud to say that I live in a valley made possible by such pioneers as these. Whenever I pass this cemetery, the headstones stand out like lonely lanterns telling me to face my problems and the future as bravely as they.

*Note:* This story won first place in a county contest and was later dramatized.

## Chewed by a Bear

John Balls and his wife Sarah, arrived in Hyde Park, Utah, in September of 1868. This was to be their new home. They had left England to join an unpopular people with an unpopular religion in the desert of the west. Hyde Park had been settled for just eight years. A few simple homes had been built, a few more were in the making, and a little rock church was being built. Timber was plentiful in the east mountains and John became interested in the lumber industry. He built a saw mill behind his house and sawed lumber for himself and his neighbors. Then the call came for him to saw lumber for the church and he was glad to oblige.

It was a fragrant June morning as John sharpened his axe preparatory to going to the canyon to cut logs. Wild roses were growing along the ditch banks and meadowlarks greeted the day with song. John was in a hurry to go. It would take him at least two hours to walk to the canyon, and the sun was already peeking over the mountains. He shoved his brown hair under his hat, tied a red handkerchief around his neck and kissed his wife goodbye. "Why don't you wait for Brother Perkes to come?" Sarah asked. "I'm afraid for you to go to the canyon alone. Suppose the bear that carried off Brother Reeder's pigs is lurking about and no one with you."

"Brother Reeder never saw the bear," John retorted. "I'm not afraid of something no one has ever seen."

"But John," she begged, "it wasn't just the pigs. The calf belonging to Brother Hurren disappeared and his dogs were mangled trying to save it. He knows he saw tracks of a bear, and a large one, too."

"I can have a tree cut down before Brother Perkes gets here, so bring me my lunch and I'll be off." John replied with pioneer determination.

John slung his axe over his shoulder, tied his canteen around his neck, and shoved his lunch of bread and honey into his pocket. Sarah watched him as he walked away whistling a tune, but fear was in her heart. "Be careful," she called again, but John paid no heed to her. He was happy as he walked along. Everything was challenging, fresh, and new in this land of America. He felt like Peter of old. "It is good to be here," he thought, "away from the chimney smoke and soot of old England." He would help to make this valley blossom.

As he ascended the canyon, the trees appeared a mottled green. Tall quaking aspen held their pale green leaves high in the sunshine, while the maples spread out in a deeper shade, and the pines clutched the mountains in the richest deep green of the forest. The whole mountainside teemed with life. Chipmunks and squirrels romped and chattered, crows fluttered in the trees, and now and then a rabbit bounced from nowhere into the thicket. About four miles up the canyon, he came to a fork in the road. Here was a cold mountain spring where he expected to fill his canteen, but what was that moving in the brush by the spring? "It's probably just the wind," he thought. He stopped to pick a wild columbine. He smelled it and tucked it in his hat band. Then the brush moved again, and before he could think, he found himself face to face with a big brown bear and two cubs. The bear gave an angry growl and made a jump at him. John dodged. He threw his lunch at the furious beast thinking the smell of honey would attract her attention. But no! The bear came and pounced upon him. He raised his axe to strike her, but the bear slapped him down and began biting his legs severely. He could feel the warm blood trickling down his ankles and smell his torn flesh. As he turned, he saw a thin froth of blood at the bear's nostrils, and blood, his blood, smeared over its mouth and chin. With another angry growl, the bear picked him up, squeezed him, and then threw him down with a hard thud.

In the meantime the cubs had run off into the thicket, and Mrs. Bear went to find them. John cried out with pain and his heart sank in dismay as he thought of being alone in the ghostly forest. What if he should die before help came? He tried to move, but he was too weak and faint from loss of blood. Then he heard a gallop in the bushes. He looked up, and the bear was back again. He was panic stricken and the pain was unbearable as the big beast chewed the fleshy part of his stomach. She mauled him in the dirt and threw him down again as she went to look for her cubs once more.

John was just half-conscious as she returned again, growling and fuming in a small furious circle. He could vaguely hear her angry snorting and he could feel her hot breath as she turned him over and shook him. With a last ray of hope, he put his hand over his face and held his breath as if he were dead. The bear smelled him and decided he was dead. She turned again to go to her cubs. She stopped suddenly and looked back, stared for a moment, then whirled and plunged into the forest.

The canyon breeze fanned John back to full consciousness. He groaned with pain. Then with an unsteady effort, he crawled down the path he had so recently traveled. To his great relief, there was Brother Perkes who had his ox team and wagon, some hay, and a couple of blankets. He made a bed for John, tied his wounds with strips of blanket, and took him home. Someone rode a horse to Logan and got Dr. Ormsby. He cared for John on and off for a year before John was able to work again. He always carried thick, ugly scars, and walked with a limp from his encounter with the bear.

Battle scars did not stop John Balls from getting lumber for the meetinghouse, however. As soon as he was able, he was cutting and sawing wood again. However, he never again went to the canyon alone.

## True Love in the Snow

George and Margaret Robinson lived a happy life in Darlington, England, with their family of six. George was an excellent cabinetmaker, a good provider for his family. In the midst of their prosperity, they heard the gospel and were all converted and baptized. Like other Latter-day Saints, they wanted to come to America, the promised land. William, the oldest son, came first. After some time, the rest of the family followed. By then, Elizabeth, the oldest daughter, was eighteen and very beautiful. She had no suitors and sought none. She was waiting until the right man came along.

The family settled in Iowa and then cast their lot with the Martin Handcart Company that was coming to Utah. It was a trying time to decide what to throw away and what to take in those little handcarts. There was the best clothing to leave, handmade lace and doilies, fancy dishes, bedding, pictures, and, in fact, almost everything that had been so dear to them.

As James, a proud boy of fourteen, saw his mother and sister crying as they threw away their prized possessions, he became bitter. "This is too much," he yelled angrily. "I will not go into that wilderness of savages and sagebrush. I am staying here."

"Have you no testimony of the gospel?" his mother asked. "After all, we came to America to join the Saints."

"I am not going," he cried angrily. "You will not find me when you start your foolish march tomorrow. I am running away." And with that, he dashed out of the house never to be seen by his mother again.

The father, who had been ill, said he could not bear to leave his youngest son among strangers, so he decided to stay with him. But resolute Margaret and her other children began the trek the next day alone. All went well the first part of the journey. There were merry times around the campfire, dancing and singing songs of praise. But winter came all too soon and the provisions gave out. They were rationed to one-fourth pound of flour per day. Many died of exposure, and Margaret, who had lived such a sheltered life and was not strong, had to be pulled by the children in the handcart every day. To add to their trials, word came that their father, George, had died.

The slow march continued, with death, hunger and fatigue ever present. Then on a dull day in October, as the company plodded along, new snows flew about them, but they forced themselves on and camped in some willows. By morning there was a foot of snow, the starving draft animals were scattered, and there were five more bodies to be buried. The ground was frozen and their strength was gone, so the survivors buried the bodies together in a snowdrift.

When the storm was over, they wallowed on toward the Sweetwater only to be halted by another storm. A night or two later, they were so worn out that nobody had strength to pitch a tent. They sat there listless, shivering and cold, resigned to their fate, but still with faith in God.

Meanwhile, missionaries bearing the news of the Martin company had reached Salt Lake City. Those assembled at October general conference heard their prophet Brigham Young abruptly adjourn the conference and call for volunteers, wagons, and supplies to go to the rescue of these unfortunate brothers and sisters. Fired with a noble sense of brotherhood, twenty-seven young men left with wagonloads of food, warm clothing, and bedding. They knew the journey would be hard, driving across snow-covered mountains, and perhaps even then they would arrive too late. Ephraim K. Hanks, who knew the country well and was a hearty and fearless scout, went ahead on horseback by himself to find the handcart company. He found them, hunted and killed a buffalo, and fed the starving people. He gave priesthood blessings, comforted and helped the suffering Saints in every way he could.

Finally the men with wagons and supplies arrived. All of the people were weak and sickly from starvation and exposure, and there were more bodies to be buried. Little children were barefoot in the snow, but now there was a ray of hope. Help had come! The rescuers built big fires, handed out food, bedding and clothing, and, as quickly as they could, loaded the weakest in wagons and started them for Salt Lake City. The strongest were still able to walk, now well-supplied with food and warm clothing.

On 30 November, the small band saw Salt Lake City for the first time. They stood on top of a mountain in snow to their waists, but the sight of Zion promised food, warmth, shelter, and a home.

Elizabeth caught sight of a strong young man, smiling as he dug through the drifts toward them. Elizabeth thought he was the most handsome man she had ever seen and, weak and hungry though she was, knew that someday she wanted to marry him. As he reached her, he stopped, took a piece of jerky from his pocket, and pressed it into her hand. His touch sent a warm wave through her cold body and brought a tint of color to her pale cheeks. The trials of the plains were forgotten deep in the snowdrifts on the high mountain. She had found love.

Within a few months, Elizabeth Robinson and Gibson Condie were married in Salt Lake City. They became the parents of a large family and settled in Preston, Idaho. None of them ever doubted the existence of love at first sight.

*Note:* This story won second place in a Sons of Utah Pioneers contest.

## Sing, Tom, Sing!

In 1866, the pioneers of western Cache Valley knew that the Indians were angry so they kept on building their fort. From time immemorial, the Indians had rejoiced in the valley's choice hunting, its grassy meadows for their ponies, its plentiful deer and rabbits for hunters, and the dense thickets of chokecherries and serviceberries that they dried for winter. Now the Mormon pioneers, determined to build new homes, challenged their possession of the land. No peaceful solution seemed possible.

The angry Indians stole their cattle, burned their wagons, and tried to climb over the fort walls. The men no longer dared go to the canyon for wood. The pioneers, under siege, decided to send for help to Mendon, a little town fifteen miles to the south. Perhaps one rider, moving fast, could get through. All the men were needed at the fort, so a young English boy named Tom volunteered to make the dangerous journey.

About sundown, he saddled his pony and put a couple of slices of bread into his pocket. His mother kissed him goodbye, holding a silent prayer in her heart that her boy would return. "Be careful," the men warned as he rode through the fort gate. "And do most of your fast riding by night."

Tom rode along trying to be brave; but as the evening shadows deepened, a flying bird, or a rabbit in the brush made him sweaty and tense. Indians might be lurking anywhere ready to grab him. Their campfires twinkled on the hillsides. The night became blacker. Tom kicked his pony's sides and urged him on faster. Suddenly there was a hoot and a swish close by his head. The pony shied, and he almost went over its head, but he regained his balance. It was only an owl. The coyote howls sent chills through his body that was fast getting numb with cold. But he kept telling himself he was riding to save his people and he must go on.

About midnight he reached Mendon and gave the alarm. Five men promised to come the next day. They urged Tom to stay and ride back with them, but knowing the anxiety of his mother, he would not. He unbridled his horse, gave him a drink, and let him munch on some grass. Then, taking a piece of bread from his pocket, he began his own dry meal. A lady, seeing his meager supper, brought him a cup of milk and a slice of cold venison which tasted mighty good.

Tom began his ride back home. He had not gone far when suddenly he was grabbed by an Indian and jerked from his horse. He tried to remain calm in spite of his fear, but he could not stop shaking, and a cold sweat covered his body.

"Will they torture me before they kill me?" Tom wondered? He could see hatred, anger, and vengeance in their painted faces, and he knew his fate was entirely in their hands.

"Indians despise a coward," thought Tom, trying to straighten his shoulders and look composed. "They must not see that I am trembling." He shoved his hands in his pockets and squirmed about on the rock. Cold beads of sweat stood on his forehead, and the Indian grins were grim and satisfied, enjoying his misery.

Longingly, Tom thought of his gentle English countryside, so different from this vast expanse of sage. Had he joined the Mormon Church only to die at the hands of savages? Well, if that was God's will, he would commend himself to God.

Humbly and fervently he offered a prayer that his life might be saved, and he had no sooner said "Amen," than he was impressed with a strong thought: "Sing! Sing, Tom! Sing!" There was no time to question this strange inspiration. In a weak and croaking voice he sang the old English song, "The Nightingale."

He hesitated, cleared his throat, and then in a stronger tenor, sang "Drink to Me Only with Thine Eyes." It seemed a burlesque to sing this song to the Indians, but in his heart, he was singing it for the lovely Danish girl, Maria, who had promised to marry him. He paused to think of her and then the prompting came again: "Sing, sing, keep singing!"

This time he sang the inspiring Mormon hymn, "Come, Come, Ye Saints." At the last verse, he faltered over, "And should we die before our journey's through, happy day! All is well!" He couldn't think of death as a happy day, especially at the hands of Indians. He lifted his head and sang, "High on a Mountain Top," looking at the mountains around him, firm and majestic, giving him the courage to continue.

Faint streaks of dawn appeared in the east. Tom drew his coat around him and was attempting one more song when the old Indian chief stood up to tell him of his fate. In deep guttural tones, he said, "One who can sing like a bird should not die. He should live to bring joy to his people."

Tom shuddered with relief. And then he heard something—a sound in the distance. He knew what it was and began singing again to cover it. But the quick ears of the Indians heard the hoofbeats. They jumped on their ponies and raced away.

In a few minutes Tom's father, with a posse, arrived to find the young man exhausted, hoarse, and shaken, but unharmed. Tom rode back to Clarkston with a testimony of the power of prayer never to be forgotten.

This singing boy became my grandfather, Thomas H. Godfrey, Jr. The words of the old Indian chief were indeed true—Grandpa brought much joy to the world with his singing. He sang at parties, concerts, funerals, and in the town choir. He bounced his grandchildren on his knee, let them hold his big silver watch, and sang to them. He sang a humorous song to the teenagers about a little drummer who loved a cross-eyed cook. Whenever there was bickering or faultfinding among his family or friends, he sang, with an English accent:

> Always hear both sides.
> Always hear both sides.
> Let equal rights all men enjoy,
> And always hear both sides.

Grandpa sang and led community singing until his death in his eighties. He never forgot the inspiration of his youth that had saved his life, "Sing, Tom! Sing!"

## Saved by a Cattail

The Indians circled around the camp of the pioneers. Their war bonnets blazed in the sun as they sat erect on their ponies, but they showed no signs of hostility. This band of Saints was cautious. The women began to hide in the wagons, gathering their little ones around them.

Suddenly there was a piercing scream. A warrior on his pony had swooped in close to a wagon and snatched up six-year-old James. In the commotion, two more Indians stole nine-year-old Shirley and rode swiftly away. There was sobbing and confusion as men grabbed their guns and tried to follow them, but the Indians knew the land and the men didn't. They hunted two days, then gave up in despair. Summer was almost over. They could not let winter trap them in the deep mountain snows.

In the camp, John and Catherine, both just sixteen, rejoiced at the birth of their first son as the company sorrowed for the lost children. The Indians didn't approach the wagon train again, but they all had that eerie feeling that they were being watched. Exhausted from their duties, tired of the monotonous diet, and grieving over the children, the people became irritable.

"Let's take the short route through the mountains," they grumbled.

"But we have been warned not to go that way," the captain cautioned. "We know there are hostile Indians there. Why take chances?"

"Let's get to our destination the quickest way," murmured the weary travelers. "We're hungry and tired. Who knows? Maybe we'll find the children if we take that road."

Against his better judgment, the captain of the wagon train was swayed by the murmurers and took the short route. The first day, all went well. The second the same. The third night as they made camp, the white canvas of the wagons shone like a streak of white clouds in the sky. Smoke streamed up from dozens of cooking fires, and the smell of roasting meat whetted already-hearty appetites. Women washed multicolored clothes and laid them on the grass and bushes to dry.

Catherine was among the women. With her brown hair flowing in the wind, she made a beautiful picture of loving motherhood as she hung her baby's clothing on the brush, carefully smoothing out each wrinkle. At sun-

**106**

down, men chopped wood for fuel and to repair wagons, and the herd boys dozed as the oxen and horses fed contentedly around them. Suddenly they heard the thud of horses' hooves and looked up to see themselves completely encircled by galloping Indians. A sudden swoop, a well-coordinated dash, and they galloped away with two women, giving savage yells. One of the kidnapped women was Catherine.

The Indians disappeared, leaving the camp in a frenzy. The air was heavy with dust as the men rode frantically after the Indians, but quickly lost their trail in the gathering darkness. As they rode sadly back into camp, the oxen stamped, and the frightened women and children sobbed.

That night no one sang "All Is Well," but prayers were offered for the missing women. With dawn, the men tried again to follow the Indians but could find no sign of them.

Terrified, Catherine had tried to wrench away from her captor and leap from his galloping horse, but he simply gripped her tighter. He laughed at her tears. "Foolish way of the white men."

When the Indians stopped to rest, they tied Catherine and the other woman with buckskin thongs, placed them far away from each other and then built a bonfire and roasted crickets. They tried to feed this savage delicacy to the women, who shook their heads, weak with nausea and fear. Catherine's breasts were aching with the milk her infant son needed. What would become of him? The thought tormented her even more than her terror about her own situation.

The embers of the fire died out. The Indians, weary from their hard ride, lay down to rest and were soon fast asleep. Catherine wriggled her hands in the bindings. Something seemed to give. Cautiously she tried again and again until one hand was free. There was not a sound. Then she untied her feet. An Indian grunted, and her heart pounded, but he turned over and continued his sleep. With a prayer to God for protection, she slipped into the underbrush. A branch cracked as she moved and again she felt all was lost, but the Indians slept on. She walked a long way in the thicket with her legs and hands cut and bleeding from the thorns.

After what seemed like hours, she came to a river. She had always feared deep water, but now it was her only hope. She slipped into the cold water and clung to some low branches. Her body shook with cold as she uttered another silent prayer to God, begging him to let her return to her husband and baby.

There was a crash in the bushes and she heard the voices of the Indians. She was frantic, but suddenly the inspiration came, "Take a cattail from the bank, lie down in the water, and breathe through it." She quickly obeyed the prompting and was under the water as the Indians searched along the bank. She lay absolutely still, knowing that the faintest ripple could betray her. Her legs cramped with cold, and fear still clutched her as she listened to the footsteps of her captors.

The Indians continued to search all that day. And all that day she remained under the water, praying for darkness to come. As the sun withdrew, so did the Indians. So cold and stiff she could hardly move, Catherine got up and forced herself to walk through the night, hoping she was headed away from the Indians and toward her friends. As morning came, she saw campfires in the east. Pioneers or Indians? She walked a little closer and saw the outline of a circle of covered wagons. It was not her own wagon train, but one that had been following behind hers. Her steps quickened. Surely these people would befriend her!

She cried out as she approached the sentries, then fell, exhausted. When she regained consciousness, the jolt of the wagon and the kind hands that bathed her fevered body helped her to know that her escape was real. Pneumonia set in, and no one thought she would live, but her prayers were answered again and she recovered.

Then one day a scout brought the word that her own wagon train was camped only a day's journey away. Catherine was so filled with joy and excitement that she could hardly be kept from running on alone.

The next day, as they approached her wagon train, men could be seen in the distance like a moving ant bed. Closer and closer, they came. Catherine could stand the suspense no longer and jumped from the slow-moving wagon and started running. Across the prairie, in the other camp, a young man stood aside, looked, hesitated, looked again, and then with a shout of joy and a bound he went to meet the eager young woman.

The men and women of both trains looked on with tears on their sunburned faces as two figures were silhouetted as one, reunited on the prairie. Moments later, a kind woman carried a tiny baby, alive and well, to the eager young mother, and her joy was complete. They were a family again.

*Note:* The other woman captured was killed trying to escape, and the two stolen children were never seen again. Catherine and her husband, John, had a total of fifteen children. She lived to be ninety-three and her husband ninety-seven. (This retold story won first place in a Sons of Utah Pioneers' contest, a gold medal, and a check for $25.)

## Spinning Wheel Hairdo

An Indian brave lurked in the trees, tired from a night of fighting and murder. He had the scalps of five white men as souvenirs of his night's plunder. He would continue to fight for his people and their hunting grounds, he told himself proudly. The whites would be driven off, or he would die bravely trying. But now he must have food.

There in a small clearing stood a cabin half-hidden by a large cedar whose branches touched the ground. Clumps of bunch grass stood up stiffly, dotting the dooryard, and a rooster high on a straw shed proclaimed the glories of the morning and another new day. Smoke came from the cabin sending little curls over the weeds on the dirt roof as it reached to touch the bright blue of the sky. It was early, and a little cold, but already the household was moving. Two little children, a boy and a girl, dashed out of the house to feed the pigs and chickens, and as they opened the door, the smell of bacon tormented the Indian's empty stomach.

He stealthily surveyed the situation. The cow had been milked, and fresh hoofprints and wagon tracks pointed to the canyon. He grinned. There would be food with no problem, and even if he did need to kill, a few more white scalps would only add to his glory. Slyly he led his horse under the cedar tree and crept softly to the door of the cabin. He pushed it open a crack and peeked in. There was a woman seated by a strange wheel that kept going round and round. He was fascinated. He stood still with wonder. Then he pushed the door inward a little more, slipped his body through the opening, and closed the door again without making a sound. He stood tall and straight with lines of bitterness and hatred showing through the war paint on his face. His shirt was streaked with blood and his coarse, black hair protruded from his war bonnet.

Sarah Jane looked up. There stood the gruesome-looking Indian warrior smiling at her. She turned white and slumped in her chair, but regained her composure as she thought of her children. She flashed her dark eyes defiantly at him, but could not utter a sound. The cords

**110**

on her neck stood out, her thin lips moved, but still no words came. She tried to rise, but found herself too weak and faint to move.

The Indian, enjoying the misery of his victim, brandished a long, thin-bladed knife and began to sharpen it on a rough piece of sandstone he held in his bloody hand. On the handle were bits of blond hair stuck with dried blood that showed through his filthy fingers. He sharpened the knife again, at the same time making tormenting grimaces toward Sarah Jane as she sat petrified at her spinning wheel.

He walked toward the crude cupboard, picked up a dish of cold mush, and began eating it with his dirty fingers. As the mush was not to his liking, he tossed the dish against the wall and laughed as it broke into little pieces. Turning next to the stove, he dipped his fingers in the greasy skillet, licked them, and proceeded to eat a piece of bacon left from the morning meal. As the heat from the stove warmed his body, a nauseating smell of sweat, blood and smoke filled the room

Sarah Jane wiped her own cold sweat on her waist apron, smoothed her dark hair, and with a prayer in her heart resumed her spinning. Round and round went the wheel as the Indian came nearer. She peeked over her shoulder and there he was, right beside her. She would die bravely she told herself, but what of her children? How could her husband stand the shock of coming home to find their butchered bodies? She prayed again as she felt the Indian's hot breath on her neck as he leaned closer to watch the magic of the spinning wheel. Closer and closer he leaned—too close! A terrified shout of pain shook the cabin. There was the chief, caught fast, his long black hair tangled with the other fibers in the spinning wheel. He stomped and roared. He swung his bloody knife, but there he was, caught fast.

The baby woke and screamed with fright at the howling of the visitor, and the children came running in from outside—terrified as they saw the redskin fighting helplessly to free himself.

Thoughts raced through Sarah Jane's mind. Shall I take my children and run and leave him here? Shall I hit him over the head with the axe? No, the Indians would kill too many whites in retaliation. Indians admire bravery. If I cut him loose, perhaps he will be friendly with the whites. She paused. I'll try kindness, she decided.

"I'm sorry, I'm sorry," cried the trembling Sarah Jane, as if he could appreciate her apologies. She took her scissors and quickly cut the strands of black hair and the Indian stood up, humiliated but free.

Meanwhile, William, who had gone to the canyon for wood, had listened to an inner voice prompting him to go home. Shaking with apprehension, he felt more anxious each step of the way. Great boulders stood in his path and he had to wind around them. The grass was slippery and dry, chipmunks skittered in the brush and crying hawks made him more tense than ever. He clucked to his horses to hurry them up the trail toward home.

As he neared the cabin, he looked suspiciously everywhere. All was quiet—too quiet. Not even the bark of the dog or the greetings of his children broke the silence. Something was wrong. He got down from his wagon and was about to enter the house when suddenly the Indian sprang from the door and made a jump for his pony, concealed behind the cedar tree. But William was too quick for him. He grabbed him by the leg and jerked him from his horse. The Indian, with the agility of a cat, dropped to his hands and tried to twist his foot away, but William held fast, sinking his fingernails into the dark skin. The Indian stood on his other foot and gave William a bunt in the stomach with his head. William staggered, but with renewed strength sent the Indian sprawling in the dirt. The savage reached for his knife. Sarah Jane and the children screamed. William, who knew he was fighting for his family, fought harder. This time he caught the red man by the throat and gripped until he began to fight for breath. His hands relaxed and the knife fell to the ground. Sarah Jane grabbed the knife and stood ready to use it, but it was not necessary—the Indian lay quietly in the dirt, the hacked ends of his black hair spread out like a matted fan. William let him breathe again and gave him a blow on the right ear for good measure. Speaking in words the Indian understood, William demanded, "If I let you go, will you promise never to molest my family again?"

The Indian promised, and William let him up. The dirt and leaves fell from his shirt as he slowly mounted his pony and rode away. But the souvenir of the fight remained. Black hair was still wound in the spinning wheel.

---

No matter how cold the nights, or how isolated we were from the outside world by the deep snow outside, stories such as these, told in the circle of our close-knit family, became woven into a pattern of memories never to be forgotten.

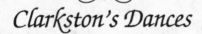

## Clarkston's Dances

Catherine H. Griffiths wrote:

When the people first settled Clarkston, they didn't have any place for public gatherings. William Stewart had the largest house in the settlement so the citizens told him that they would put in a lumber floor if he would let them use it for dances. This he did and the dancing began. Later they danced in a log building used for school and church and then in the rock meetinghouse.

The dances began at dusk and lasted until two or three or even four o'clock in the morning. Refreshments were served at midnight. During dances special stunts were performed such as step dancing by Joseph Louis Thompson and the sword dance by Andrew W. Heggie. Then there were songs, speeches, etc. Joseph and Oscar Myler were the first musicians and played for many years.

When our little rock meetinghouse was constructed, it presented a prim Sunday appearance with its benches arranged in two neat rows and rag runners in the aisles. A black, coal stove stood in the middle of the floor with its long pipe going straight up through the ceiling. On dance nights, the carpet was rolled up, and the benches were piled high in the corner of the hall. The four chandeliers, each with four kerosene lamps, smoked and sputtered unnoticed by the happy crowd.

I'm glad I didn't live in the age of babysitters. My parents always took us to the dances. Sometimes we were tired and uncomfortable, but it was fun.

A long row of benches turned facing together on the stand made a community bed for the children. There, with coats for pillows and more coats for covers, we snored, wiggled, or coughed in the dust. Occasionally, a parent would come up, look us over, then turn some sleeping offender who had managed to get his feet in another's face. Sometimes the caller became overwrought if the dancers became confused, and in his excitement raised his voice and woke some of us up.

This was the day of square dancing, but the hot debate was already underway on the issue of whether the waltz was decent. Some said, "The idea of holding another man's wife in your arms! How could such a thing be approved of?" Those who suggested a waltz were thought bold, very bold, and perhaps immodest. The waltz remained taboo.

I pulled myself up from my bed on the bench and watched the dancers do the scottische to the tune "Have You Seen My New Shoes?" Then there was the polygamists' dance. They danced in sixes—two pairs of one man and two women—then passed on through where a new set was formed. The tune was in a minor key, and it sounded sad and melancholy as the caller sang "Balance on the Corner." But the dancers laughed, so I thought everyone must be happy.

The dance manager called out, "The crowd is so big tonight, we'll have to give each man a number. The even numbers will dance first and then the odd." This met with no objection, for dancing was a thoroughly democratic activity. Women looked forward to dancing with every man in the hall. Weight and halitosis were no objection, and what a friendly spirit this made.

I noticed how gracefully the women could promenade, their full skirts flowing out but never exposing an ankle. I watched Uncle Sam swing his partner, knees together and arms straight out and stiff. Then there was John T. who had an odd little hop that reminded me of a rooster as he turned the corner.

Finally, sleep overcame me, but I managed to wake up for the last dance, always "Home, Sweet Home," to see who was taking whom home. It was perfectly proper for a girl to come to the dance alone and be escorted home by the man to whom she granted the last dance. The dance closed with prayer and the sleeping kids were carried home.

A favorite story among the old folks of our town was one about the square dance caller, Bill Flinders. Bill sang his calls to the music of the orchestra. One night he looked down and saw his sister, Jane, going the wrong direction in the square. He sang out excitedly, "Oh damn you, Jane, why don't you cross over and take that young man by the humptedy dumptedy." People laughed so hard that the dance stopped while Jane took her proper place. It must have been hilarious, because in telling the story, the old folks still laugh until the tears run down their cheeks.

I often wonder what the good old brethren who fought so tenaciously against the waltz would think about today's dancers. Cheek to cheek dancing, bare toes with bright red polish emerging from open sandals, backless dresses, bare shoulders, lipstick, rouge, eye shadow, the same partner all evening, loud clapping, and encores. What celestial beard-pulling and frowns there must be!

## Fashion Finds Us

"You must come to the dance with us tonight, Edith," Mother called from the stove.

"Yes, I just love to fox-trot," answered Edith, our eighteen-year-old glamorous cousin from California.

"But they don't allow that here," my brother chipped in. "We just waltz and two-step." (By this time the waltz was acceptable.)

"What's wrong with the fox-trot?" Edith queried, as she began to sing and demonstrate the fox-trot in our big kitchen.

"I don't know," Mother answered serenely. "The bishop just won't allow it." We had all seen it. Any unknowing visitor who danced the fox-trot was put humiliatingly off the floor. If he clapped for two encores, the floor manager would yell, "Only one encore in this town."

Edith had tried to be polite, but she hadn't been able to refrain from dropping a few hints at how old-fashioned we were. Now her eyebrows rose. She swooped down on each of us in turn, teaching us the fox-trot so fashionable in California and so taboo in our little town.

That evening, we clustered around Edith in awe as she got ready. I held the mirror by the kerosene lamp, as she pencilled her eyebrows. From a neat little white case, she daubed pink coloring on her cheeks, then smeared something greasy and red over her lips from a tube. My passionate loyalty to my beautiful cousin wavered. I felt embarrassed to take her to our dance with a painted face. And I was downright ashamed of her dress, with hardly any sleeves! What would our townspeople say?

As we neared the meetinghouse, we could hear my uncle playing "Over the Waves" on his fiddle with cornet, clarinet, and piano accompanying the melody as they had for a generation. Edith suppressed a little snicker. "No drums? No saxophone?" We stared at her. Drums were for parades—or jungles.

All eyes turned toward her when we walked in. Here was a city girl, a real live painted doll! Whispers ran around the hall. Mother asked an uncle to come and meet Edith. He acted a little shy, said, "Pleased to meet you," and asked for the next dance. The orchestra struck up "When You Wore a Tulip," and everyone began to two-step with vim. As the orchestra neared the chorus, my uncle popped a fiddle string. After losing about three counts, the cornet bravely took over the melody and the dancers got back in step.

Edith was the center of attraction, but she liked that. She had large, blue eyes. They passed dismissively over the other girls but lingered languorously on the young men who stared back, fingered their ties, and stepped forward to ask her to dance.

I had heard about jealousy, but now I saw it before my fascinated eyes. One woman said it was an insult to God when he had already made her beautiful to defile herself with paint. Another called her a "low-down, city hussy." Yet down deep, I could see she was the envy of all.

Low necks, short sleeves, and make-up had been introduced to Clarkston once and for all. Slowly the mutiny began. Some of our young men drove their horses and sleighs into Smithfield to see just what a dance in the outside world was like. They came back aglow—but to their elders, it was fireworks. The young folks passed cutting judgment on our faithful old orchestra. Its members, who had played free on every community occasion, were hurt. There were bitter words and tears. Neighbors jangled. The young folks sulked and wouldn't dance. Finally, some of our leaders drove to Newton to look in on a "modern" dance and capitulated.

The young folks won. But did they? We had new dance bands that drove in for the evening. How you felt about jazz determined your social class. And the good old dances of the past, where a man boasted of dancing with every woman in the hall, became a memory.

## Clarkston's First Baby

When I called on Aunt Annie H. Jardine, age ninety-two, I found her living with her daughter. She had just finished crocheting on a lovely pair of pillow cases. Bright in mind and eager to tell me of the early days in Clarkston, she began by telling me that she was born in a dugout to Andrew Heggie and Annie Stewart Heggie in 1868, the first child born in Clarkston. One of her first memories was to look up out of the dugout and see some men carrying a crude casket containing the body of Penelope Thompson to be buried in the first grave in Clarkston. "I have watched that graveyard grow to what it is at present," she said, with sad memories flooding her mind.

Then she told me of seeing Martin Harris, his frail body and his white hair. She said that people were kind

118

to this important little man and loved to gather and hear him bear his testimony of the truthfulness of the Book of Mormon.

She was in Salt Lake City attending conference, 5 April 1876, when the great explosion at the arsenal near Ensign Peak occurred. The panic-stricken people, the broken windows, dishes falling from cupboards, dirt flying, and debris everywhere made an impression on her young mind never to be forgotten.

Then I asked a very poor question. "What was your trousseau like when you got married?"

"Trousseau?" she gasped disgustedly. "I had no trousseau. No one thought of any finery in those days." She recounted her trip in a wagon to Logan, Utah, to be married in the temple to James B. Jardine. John P. Clark and Sarah Homer, another engaged couple traveled with them. They stayed all night with friends and returned home the next day with the few pieces of furniture they could afford.

Then I made another mistake. "What were some of your wedding presents?" I asked Sister Jardine. She was shocked and I was embarrassed.

"Wedding presents!" she exclaimed. "Nobody could give wedding presents. We did well to keep alive."

Aunt Annie reared a family of nine, and they in turn have taken care of her in her old age. She is tired now and has no regrets when she thinks of rejoining her loved ones and leaving her mortal remains in the graveyard she has watched grow from the beginning of Clarkston.

## Stab the Villain!

Clarkston enjoyed its own home theatricals, which enlivened the long winter months. In one play, the hero was supposed to shoot the villain. He pulled the trigger at the fatal moment, but the gun would not work. There were a few agonizing moments of delay, and he tried again and failed again. All the characters stepped around wondering what to do next. Finally, Emily Griffin called out, If the gun won't go off, stab him. This ad lib caused more fun than the play.

## Grandma Had a Beau

A young black-haired Englishman walked all the way from Salt Lake City out to Millcreek to be with me at Sunday School. He ate dinner with our family and also stayed for meeting.

This entry in the diary of Mary Helen Scott, my grandmother, does not record the name of the young Englishman, but it was Peter S. Barson, my grandfather. Mary Helen's father was a polygamist and at the same dinner table was Rebecca, the sixteen-year-old daughter of another mother, who promptly set her cap for Peter. Mary Helen was torn. Rebecca had always been her favorite sister. They had tended babies together, milked the cows, and pulled flax until their hands were cut and bleeding from the sharp blades. Now that they were sixteen, they practiced the promenade, balancing apples on their heads to develop grace and smoothness. Mary Helen knew there would never be a sister quite like Rebecca. But her heart also told her that Peter was the one for her.

On Peter's next call, he walked up the lane toward the Scott home as the little children called out, "Here comes the city slicker, here comes the city slicker." Rebecca, who loved practical jokes, saw him near the log across Millcreek and untied their feisty ram. The ram promptly braced himself at the other end of the log and eyed Peter with a wicked gleam. Peter felt a little nervous but could not back down or "coward" would join "city slicker." He cautiously moved along the log. The children were laughing as they looked on. He stretched out his hand toward the ram and made soothing noises as he took another step. The ram stood still. He felt a little braver and took two more steps, never taking his eyes from the animal.

"Watch out, Pete," the children yelled. The ram lunged forward, head down, and bunted Peter sprawling into the creek. He dragged himself onto the bank feeling sheepish in every sense of the word. The children were still laughing as Rebecca, with profuse apologies, found him some of Ephraim's clothes and offered to hang his wet ones to dry. Peter managed to hold his temper exceptionally well, but he would have liked to slap all the kids and shake Rebecca.

Rebecca was charming for the rest of his visit; but on his next visit, Peter brought two homemade rings for Mary Helen. One had been made from the back of an old comb that he had melted and shaped to fit her finger and the other from a large broken hair pin he had found. Each had been polished with meticulous care, and he could not hide his pride as he presented them to his sweetheart. Rebecca understood the message and silently wept. The evening passed quickly and Mary Helen noticed Rebecca's red eyes as John Scott called his family and four young men visiting various daughters together for their evening prayer. She was proud and happy to have Peter kneel by her side in prayer, but her kind heart ached for Rebecca.

Father Scott, the autocrat, called upon another suitor present to offer prayer, and Peter secretly enjoyed the young man's embarrassment as he stumbled through a prayer. Suddenly he thought, what if his turn was next? That wouldn't be so funny. He resolved to memorize a righteous-sounding prayer, one that would impress John Scott.

John Scott announced sternly, "The doors of my house will be locked at nine o'clock." The four visiting suitors looked at the clock, quickly found their hats, shook hands with the entire family, and departed.

Thanksgiving time came, and Cousin Hannah came from Provo to spend a few days at the Scott home. Hannah was pretty, skilled in feminine wiles, and amused by taking beaux away from any girl. The trusting Mary Helen didn't sense her danger. She recorded in her diary, "I made me a pair of shoes to go to the Thanksgiving dance with Peter." But she danced little; Hannah monopolized Peter who was flattered by the glamorous cousin's attention and responded with wit and fun. Mary Helen sat sadly on the bench, watching Hannah bring out the best in him. The dance finally ended and Peter accompanied the girls to the Scott home. Hannah gloated, while Mary Helen sat silent and drooping, and Rebecca felt unspoken sympathy.

Aunt Sarah Ellen, the third wife, seeing Mary Helen's suffering said, "Fight for him, you ninny. I'll do your chores anytime you want to go courtin', and you can wear my white petticoat with the embroidered ruffle." Mary Helen made no response. Seeing that this offer didn't work, Aunt Sarah Ellen opened the lid of a wooden box that had been neatly covered with a brown calico print and extracted a length of bright green paisley. "See," she said, "this is a piece of goods my brother brought me from California. I will make a dress for you. I'll make it with puffed sleeves and a bustle and—." The smile she had been waiting for came. "Now go and get your man."

With this encouragement and the confidence brought by a pretty dress, Grandma caught her beau, and she wrote next in her diary, "I am engaged to be married." Her trousseau was simple. She earned enough money for two factory nightgowns. Her brother Hyrum shot hawks for her, and she picked enough soft feathers from them to make a feather bed. She tried to teach Peter to say Mary Helen, but he clung to his English accent, and she was still "Mary Ellen." Obliging as always, she changed her name to Mary Ellen to avoid further embarrassment.

Peter had saved three hundred dollars. He worked for Wells Fargo, changing horses as the fast stagecoaches came through. With no parents or home, he decided to give his money to Mary Ellen for safekeeping. Several days later, he thought, "Suppose Mary Ellen should run off with some other man. What then would become of my money?" The thought of losing that money worked on Peter's mind for several days; until, in desperation, he walked to Millcreek and asked Mary Ellen to give back his money. She was hurt, but did as he asked. A few days later, Peter was sent north with freight to Corinne, then a "gentile" city, notorious for its gambling.

As Peter jolted along the dusty road, he noticed the new homes in the valley. There was progress on every hand. Orchards were growing; shade trees, lilacs, honeysuckle, golden glow, and yellow roses were planted around many of the homes—even his perennial favorite, hollyhocks. Surely God was with his people.

But often Peter felt mixed up. Could Mormonism be true when it had taken his all? His mother and sisters had died with cholera at St. Louis enroute to Utah. His father had died shortly after their arrival in the valley, and his stepmother had apostatized, sold the old home, and gone East. He thought of the day he watched her leave. He was just twelve. She had handed him fifty cents, climbed in the stagecoach, and left him to face life on his own. Did God watch over his children? He wasn't sure. Sometimes a reckless surge swept over him! What did anything matter? There was no one to care.

But there was Mary Ellen and the testimony of his father that he could never get away from. It came to him at night, at his work, wherever he was; always it came, "My boy, Mormonism is true, but don't be deceived by the way some people live it." No, he would not be deceived.

He stopped to water his horses, and eat the boiled egg and the piece of bread he had brought for lunch. Soon he would be eating Mary Ellen's Yorkshire pudding and gooseberry pie. He would raise some pigs and there would be big slices of ham. He would never be hungry again.

It was dusk as he neared Corinne. He had traveled in the dust all day, and the lights he saw meant food, water and rest. The smells of alkali and swamp grass mixed with horse sweat penetrated his dust-plugged nostrils. He cracked his whip and urged his tired horses on. Music from the bar-rooms floated out to the dusty streets; and as he looked through the windows, everyone seemed to be having a good time.

While he stood gaping, a sociable stranger took him by the arm and said genially, "Howdy, stranger. How about me and you havin' a good time tonight? I suppose you have a little money?" How proud Peter was to say that he did, and he was at once a member of the excited crowd, with his newly found friend always suggesting something more. The jolly, friendly man encouraged him to spin the "Wheel of Fortune." "Right this way," he called out. "Come and get rich overnight."

Round and round and round she goes
And where she stops nobody knows.

Peter tried the wheel several times; but each time it stopped, his money was in the wrong place. He shook dice, and he played cards trying to make more money, but he always lost. As morning broke, Peter counted his money. He had thirty dollars left. Shame and humiliation crept over him. How could he get married now, and what would Mary Ellen think of such a fool? He walked out alone along the banks of Bear River, sat down, took out his red handkerchief, and wept bitter tears of self-condemnation.

After returning to Salt Lake City, he walked again to Millcreek and told Mary Ellen his story. The loyal girl told him that she loved him just as much with thirty dollars as with three hundred, and they would be married just as they had planned.

Peter asked the consent of Mother Scott to marry her daughter, but John Scott was not at home. It would not do to marry without his consent, so Peter sent a telegram. John Scott replied, "I will give my approval if first you get the consent of Brigham Young."

Peter ripped up the telegram and said, "The old son-of-a-bitch. It was bad enough to have to be bothered with Mr. Scott."

But John Scott was an absolute monarch in his own home, and Peter knew he would have to see Brigham Young. A few days later, Peter, decked out in his Sunday best, knocked at the office door of the president. A man that looked almost square in stature with sandy hair and beard, keen gray eyes, and a kindly smile looked out at him. Peter was surprised to hear President Young ask, "So you are the son of the late Samuel Barson, the singer?"

"Yes, sir," Peter began to feel more at ease. "I want to get married and I must have your consent to please John Scott."

President Young smiled as he said, "You are ready to get married? Well, go my boy, and may God bless you." He took a gold-colored pencil from his pocket and wrote on a piece of paper. "I give my consent to this marriage. Brigham Young." The interview that Peter dreaded so much turned out to be a pleasant one. He left the office feeling more important. The busy president knew him and had been watching him.

At last he would have a home of his own, someone to laugh with, and someone to love—his own Mary Ellen.

## My Turn

I taught second grade in Logan when I was eighteen years old and was paid the grand salary of $55 a month. Of course I still went home to Clarkston whenever I could. That was the year Grover Goodsell set me up for a blind date with Joseph Hansen. Grover and his betrothed, Maude, brought Joseph to my house in a horse and buggy. Traveling from the little town of Newton to Clarkston—less than five miles—was a considerable distance in those days. My brothers peeped through the keyhole when they arrived, not wanting to miss a minute of the excitement.

Joseph and I courted for two years. The second year I came back to Clarkston and taught first grade. We were married in 1920 in the Logan temple and moved into an old rock house in Newton. We soon decided we wanted to be on our own and moved to Dayton, Idaho and bought a farm. I continued to teach school there.

## Old Folks' Party

An Old Folks' Party was an annual affair that broke the monotony of a long winter. It was not a party for the aged but for every married couple; and with our town boasting only few unmarried over twenty, it might better be thought of as a ward party without the kids.

The committee changed little, from year to year. Aunt Lucy Ann Jensen, who was an authority on eats, supervised the dinner. She could tell you how many pounds of butter and how many loaves of bread it would take for the party. She knew who made the best bread, whose butter wasn't strong, and whose cakes weren't heavy. She parceled out assignments to the women accordingly. Sometimes feelings resulted, but they were usually submerged in the festivities of the day.

Danish Grandma Godfrey always made the coffee. She enjoyed the drink frankly and suffered no remorse of conscience from Church prohibitions against it. She always maintained, and I'm sure she sincerely believed it, that "coffee was good for folks. With plenty of sugar and lots of rich cream, coffee won't hurt anybody." Her well-appreciated skills were employed for this party until the stake president said it was sacrilegious for Mormons to serve this drink and preach against it. Then we turned to punch.

The dinner committee gathered the food and had it ready to serve promptly at twelve o'clock. In the meantime, the table committee gathered saw-horses and planks and created two long tables running the length of the hall, spread with tablecloths and decorated with the town's finest geraniums. The oldest members of the ward were seated at the head of the table near the bishop who gave the blessing on the food. With toasts and plenty to eat, all were in a jovial mood for the program.

The program was also a ritual. The committee had the bishop read assignments for it in sacrament meeting a week before the event took place. No one was ever contacted personally, and no one refused. Someone read a poem called, "Alaska," which all knew by heart. Bertha Ravsten read a comic paper which she called "Current Events" with jokes on local people. Brother Bengt Ravsten sang the verses of "Hard Times Come Again No More" and all joined in the chorus.

If the prepared program didn't last long enough,

people felt free to call for their favorite numbers. "Let's have Jim Godfrey sing 'Noah's Ark,'" called one. "Fetch him out," roared the audience, clapping. Warm and embarrassed, Jim stepped to the stand, cleared his throat, hummed a few measures and let them have it:

> The animals marched in two by two,
> From the polar bear to the kangaroo.
> And they all felt jolly and gay
> When Noah came marching in.

Uncle Billy Clark was a favorite singer, and Effie Barson put us all in a reflective mood as she sang, "We're Growing Old Together." Then it was time to do chores and get back for the dance at night, where the town orchestra always played free as their contribution to the day.

After three hours of dancing, we waded home through snowdrifts, warmed by the sociability and filled with gratitude for living in such a wonderful town.

## The Ace of Spades

Although card playing was frowned upon by the more devout members of our town as symbols of the devil, these stiff pasteboard rectangles provided a lot of fun during the dull winter days. Card parties were surprises "given on" a family chosen quite spontaneously by their neighbors.

A sleighful, or even two, would arrive to spend the day and part of the night. The men unhitched the horses and fed them, while the housewife bustled into the parlor with paper and kindling, starting a fire in the parlor heater that hadn't been used since the last time company came. The guests sat huddled in their coats and mittens while cold drafts and stale odors issued from the old heater's cracklings, smokings, and sputterings. More coal was piled in the kitchen range, and the women and children took turns sitting on the oven door. As the house began to warm, the coats and diaper bags were piled high on the best bedroom bed. Whenever the door opened, a frigid gush of wind, straight from the North Pole, blew in.

Surveying the size of her crowd, the housewife would next hastily pull a ham from a barrel of brine in the cellar or call her husband to get the axe and chop a generous roast from the frozen critter hanging from the rafters in the granary.

Then she quickly checked the bread box. If it wasn't bulging, she silently counted noses for soda biscuits. Vegetables were easy. A large cabbage, its dirty, moldy outer leaves pulled away, joined withered, spongy carrots soaking in a pan of water to plump up enough to peel. Volumes of steam and smoke from scorched ends of meat cooking filled the room.

The dessert of choice was a roly-poly pudding. A rich dough flattened into a rectangle was spread with thick blue plum preserves and rolled up, the ends pinched firmly to hold in the jam. Then the good wife would put the roll into a white cloth bag and drop it into a kettle of boiling water. Cooked to the right consistency, it was served in slices with cream and sugar. It was a real doughy delicacy, unsurpassed by modern desserts.

With dinner underway in the kitchen, the card playing began in earnest, the men standing the women with the understanding that the losers would wash the dishes.

One particular day the women had walloped the men so badly they decided that in addition to doing the dishes, the men must also churn the butter. Grandpa Barson was sent to get the cream but instead slipped a mixture of flour and water into the churn. Splash, splash, up and down went the dasher. After an hour, Uncle Jim decided there must be something wrong with the cream.

He lifted the lid and soon saw why butter hadn't come. He knew at once where to place the blame.

"Pete, you old fool," he cried. "To think of knowing you and still working the way I have."

Everyone enjoyed the joke and resumed the card playing. This time, they decided, the losers would prepare supper, and anyone who found fault with the meal should do the dishes. It fell to John Buttars to make the soda biscuits. By accident—he said—he doubled the necessary amount of soda. The biscuits came out a tempting gold; but Grandpa took one bitter mouthful, pulled a wry face, choked, and said, "These damned things—" then thought quickly "—ought to be good for heartburn." The crowd laughed, and someone suggested calling in the dogs and the pigs. All agreed but were dubious about the animals' appreciation for the generous meal.

The fires burned low. Cold drafts and frost began to sneak in around the window frames and doors. Victors and vanquished reluctantly agreed to resume the contest another time.

Cold coats were brought from the bedroom, the women did a last bit of visiting, and the men brought round the sleighs. Sometimes the cows were milked late that night, but milked they always were, for no self-respecting man would allow a high-producing cow to suffer long.

## Aunt Caroline

Aunt Caroline was a tall dignified woman. She wore a heavy, black net over her bob and always spoke in authoritative tones. If she said, "You children go now," never one word of sass or the thought of calling her an old so-and-so crossed your mind. You just went.

Aunt Caroline had been set apart by the bishop to help with the healing of the sick, and we all respected her in that holy calling. She used the remedies of the day and called in the priesthood when she thought it necessary to invoke the help of a higher power.

She delivered my brother Seth; and as a little chap he delighted her by saying, "Aunt Caroline bought me and selled me to us."

After one birth, my mother had a gathered breast (inflammation). She had been ill most of the winter and we had all become quite discouraged. Aunt Caroline called and applied hot beeswax poultices. A day of this treatment brought no improvement, so she decided a hot pancake might bring the pus to a head so it could be lanced. Accordingly, she mixed some pancake batter, fired up the coal stove, and heated the frying pan just hot enough to fry a tempting brown pancake. Oh, the smell of that pancake! And to think it was to be used for a poultice instead of going into my watering mouth! I thought longingly of how it would taste spread with butter and peach jam.

I looked on as she applied the pancake. Then she sat down by Mother, took her hand, and sang all the verses of "Count Your Many Blessings," starting with:

When upon life's billows you are tempest tossed,
When you are discouraged thinking all is lost,
Count your many blessings, name them one by one,
And it will surprise you what the Lord has done.

Her voice was off key, but a tear wet my cheek. Somehow I felt a little nearer to the angels that day.

The pancake remedy was very effective. The infection was drawn to the surface so it could be lanced and Mother rapidly recovered.

# Open Winter

The happy news of the 1918 victories during World War I reached our town. There were Chateau Thierry, St. Mihiel, and the Argonne Forest. Our spirits were high for we knew the war would soon be over and our dough-boys would be back on the farm for next summer. We heard that there was a bad flu going around, but we barely paid attention to it. It seemed so far away, and we felt remote from it all until a telegram came saying one of our own soldiers was near death with that flu at an army hospital. The whole town was upset. We prayed until another telegram came saying he was out of danger.

The dreaded flu moved closer and closer, and still none of us were stricken. But to be more safe, we all wore white masks, like those worn in the operating room, tied securely around our faces. All public gatherings were prohibited. Even those who found school dull were bored at being confined to home, and people who never stepped inside the church said, "Doesn't it seem funny with no meetings on Sunday?" It was a boring fall.

Our only excitement was in November when we heard that the armistice was signed. Then small boys got on their ponies and dragged tin cans through the streets. Someone tolled the school bell, mothers wept for joy, and the flag was raised on the public square.

Our rejoicing was short-lived. As Christmas neared with no snow, the wise of the town began to say, "A black Christmas means a black graveyard," followed by, "An open winter means an open graveyard. You just wait and see. There is no snow or ice to kill the germs in the air. We'll pay for this."

January came. There was little visiting and no loitering at the stores or post office. Fear of an unseen monster pervaded the air, and all was gloom. It was a welcome respite when two of our young people decided to get married.

On the night of the party, the young folks took off their masks and had an evening of gaiety to be remembered. They played "barnyard," and while the show-off of the crowd was up crowing, someone put an egg on his chair. The young couple opened their presents. The happiness was like a medicine.

But within a week, the groom was seriously ill with flu. People did not dare go in to help the family, so finally Bishop Ravsten said, "Surely the Lord will protect me," and went. Every day as he came down the street to go home, people came outside to ask how the young man was.

Then as if struck by a bomb, the whole town had flu. Sometimes one immune sibling cared for the other members of the family, but more often the entire family was bedfast simultaneously. Dr. Eliason came out from Logan, but all he could do was tell us to keep warm and let the disease run its course.

Then the deaths began. Little Rhea Larsen died of pneumonia. The few able-bodied dug the grave and Mr. Lindquist came out from Logan and prepared the body for burial. Sick people mourned in their beds, and the small number who were well attended the outdoor funeral services.

Our two stores were out of medicine, lemons, and oranges. Two volunteers, Virgil Atkinson and Will Shepherd, went from house to house every day, taking orders, then drove to Trenton for mustard, cough syrup, lemons, and soup bones. They paid for these commodities out of their own pockets, taking their chances that they would be repaid. Bishop Ravsten visited every stricken home, bringing food and medicine. Often he kept all-night vigil, night after night, at a sickbed.

The next to go was Esther Buttars, a young woman in the full blossom of womanhood. She had been vibrant and vigorous, not frail or sickly. Who would be next? We mourned with raging fevers and aching heads.

I remember the nauseating smell of fever mixed with mustard plasters, slop jars, bed pans, and broth. Homes lacked bathrooms and furnaces, so as many as three beds were placed in one little room near a hot blast heater. The few who were well grew desperately tired from doing chores, cooking, and nursing all day and all night. Hearing of our plight, some of the women from Trenton came up and gladdened many homes with their help.

The bishop administered to the sick and admonished us to accept the will of God without murmur. What strength he gave. In our human way, we tried to say, "Thy will be done," and then death struck Albert Griffin, the father of five children. The melancholy and gloom were almost more than a sick town could bear.

Another week passed. Faithfully Will and Virgil delivered supplies daily to every home, traveling both to Logan on the east and Downey on the north to get what was needed. The majority of people began to feel better, and as soon as they were able, they visited the homes of the bereaved, each recounting the sickness in his own family. The trouble shared somehow seemed less grievous to bear.

By February, school reopened and church began again. What joy to meet people once more and what a spiritual uplift to sing "God Moves in a Mysterious Way." We had been chastened and humbled in an unforgettable manner.

And then it snowed. Drifts piled high; fences and roadways were covered. We were snowbound, but that wasn't like being bedfast. Folks said, "The snow will kill the germs, and we will all be well again." We looked at the drifts and were happy.

## A Rag Bee

A rag bee was a highlight for Clarkston's women during its long winter evenings. With a group of chattering friends, sewing briskly by the light of a sputtering, stinking, coal oil lamp, sometimes you could make ten balls of rags in one evening.

The hostess would issue invitations and prepare her refreshments with care. When the guests had arrived and the preliminary visiting was over, she began the affair by emptying a large sack of rags torn into inch-wide strips in the middle of the room. The rags breathed the conglomerated odors of mold, raw onions, unventilated bedrooms, and homemade soap, but no one seemed to mind. Each lady vied with her neighbor to see who could make the biggest ball in the shortest length of time, sewing the strips end to end; but, of course, the real business of the evening was "catching up on the news" or the time-honored practice of gossiping.

Clarkston gossip had its rules. It was not considered modest to speak of pregnancy in front of unmarried girls, and to ask a woman when she expected a baby was the height of all rudeness. The sick of the ward, new recipes for bread pudding, and the futility of girls leaving home to go to school provided plenty to talk about.

Tongues wagged and needles flew until about nine o'clock, when it was time for refreshments. Each guest washed her hands in the tin wash basin and then rubbed them with butter preparatory to the candy pull. Gobs of bitter and brown molasses, boiled to the hard ball stage, were passed to each one and the stretching began until the candy was white and brittle.

About ten o'clock, chattering friends waded home

through the snow where the glow of a pleasant evening warmed a clammy bed in a cold room.

When the hostess had enough balls of rags, she took them to the weaver and chose the bright-colored warp for her carpet. Then at house cleaning time in the spring, there was a new carpet to be tacked down over fresh straw for the crackling pleasure of the whole family.

## Surprise!

Faithful Grandpa Barson (Sanko) described this surprise party during the winter of 1898 for the Logan *Journal:*

> A grand surprise was held in the meetinghouse in honor of Brother Joseph E. Myler who has conducted the choir for the past 18 years. Mr. Myler had previously requested the choir members to be present on Tuesday evening for the purpose of holding a general practice. In the meantime William Clark, Agnes Shumway, and Emma Dahle acting as a visiting committee, had invited the members of the ward to convene at the meetinghouse a half hour earlier than the time set for the practice.
>
> Tables were loaded with good things to eat and drink. Brother Myler's feelings when he learned of the mammoth surprise being given in his honor may more easily be imagined than described.
>
> He finally recovered sufficiently to thank his neighbors and friends for the respect shown him. After which all sat down and ate a hearty meal. Following came a program of vocal and instrumental music, recitations, speeches, and step dances. In the latter exercise Bishop Jardine and Counselor Heggie acquitted themselves with great agility, as did Bro. Myler and Sister Jardine in the Highland Fling. We danced until twelve o'clock and all went home happy through the crisp winter night.

## Grandpa's Party

Dad hitched up the horses and pulled the sleigh up close to the house to wait for us. We all walked in circles with excitement getting ready, for we were going to Grandpa Barson's for a party. We pulled on the black woolen mittens that Grandma Barson had knitted us for Christmas and buckled our overshoes. We took some hot rocks out of the oven and put them in old woolen socks to keep our feet warm on our journey. The boys pulled their ear pads down over their ears, and I tied my white silk scarf securely under my chin. Mother bundled the baby in a heavy black and gray fringed shawl and covered his face with a diaper so the wind wouldn't take his breath as we stepped out. Dad carried quilts to put under us and more to put over us. Then we cuddled down in the clean yellow straw and were off.

Occasionally, we would peek out from under the quilts as we went down a big snow bank or hit a rut in the road. Our anticipation was high as we wondered what new games we would play or who Grandpa would call out for the impromptu program. No one ever said "no" to what he asked them to do. "No" didn't go with Grandpa. He was always up and coming and insisted that his offspring be the same.

After a half hour's ride, we stopped at the big front porch of Grandpa's farm house. He helped us unload, little ones first and on up according to age. Our quilts were piled on the mahogany staircase of the big hall, and our rocks were taken to the kitchen to be warmed again for our return journey.

With our wraps put away, we were ready for the kissing ceremony that always took place going and coming. Grandpa demanded that everyone but his sons-in-law line up in a row and kiss him. I can still feel the sharp sting of his mustache as I went through the procession. I always hid and rubbed my mouth when the ordeal was finished, but I sensed Grandpa's pride. The kisses were his own way of saying, "I love you. You choice descendants are mine, all mine."

The children assembled in the big parlor where the chandelier was lighted and a fire was burning in the hot blast heater. This big parlor, open only on special occasions, always fascinated me. The heavy woodwork was painted white and trimmed with gold to match the wallpaper, and the plush carpet had dazzling red roses on a background of green. Thick lace curtains that smelled of flour starch, were draped over the big bay window, and directly in front of it stood a little round table with glass ball feet. On it was spread a piece of Grandma's netting, the big family Bible, and two worn albums of family pictures. The old organ was weighed down with images, doilies, vases of paper flowers, shells, and glass paper weights. Enlarged photographs of dead ancestors peered from every corner of the room, sometimes enthralling me and sometimes making me feel uncomfortably under surveillance. I used to sit on a chair with my feet dangling down and watch the odd-shaped crystals dangle from the chandelier. I knew better than to put my feet on the chair round, or I'd be called a "country jake" with no manners. I stood the discomfort pleasantly, feeling that no other ten-year-old girl could boast a grandpa with such a parlor.

All of my cousins arrived, and the children's dance began. Aunt Bessie at the organ patiently helped Uncle Hyrum tune his fiddle and Uncle Bird his bass viola. Grandpa as caller began, "Circle all, first to the right, then to the left and everybody bow."

By this time, several of the smaller children had to be

lifted to their feet, but there were no quitters. "Swing your partners and promenade all." And we were off again. As the dance ended, LaRee and I always begged for a two-step and our orchestra obliged with "Red Wing." Over the big red roses we danced, always careful to miss the rug or the big dog that could open his mouth.

Then we waltzed to "Over the Waves" and "After the Ball." Most of the family could play by ear; when one gave out pumping the organ, another was summoned, and the dance went on.

Then came the supper with the table spread out the full length of the dining room. There was thick black currant pie made by Aunt Eliza, Aunt Effie's mahogany cake, Aunt Mattie's salad, Aunt Annie's lemon pie, and Mother's biscuits. A party would not be complete without Grandma's fried cakes (doughnut batter twisted into a figure eight and deep-fried) and homemade ice cream—sometimes flavored only with a little salt, but that didn't matter.

With our stomachs crammed, the children went back to the parlor games while our mothers did the dishes. Grandpa passed each a handful of beans, and we played "Auction." He had wrapped several trinkets from his last trip to Logan for this occasion, and we were to bid with our beans.

"What am I offered for this prize?" he would ask, holding up a package. We knew that its size could be very misleading. "Two beans, not enough. Someone make it six. Four I'm offered, someone make it six. Sold to the highest bidder for six beans." Sylvia came forward and found her prize to be a boiled egg cup. The game continued until every child was the proud owner of a fancy button hook, a mug, or an image.

The clothes rack behind the heater drying the thick, canton flannel diapers of several babies began to give off a pungent odor. In came Grandpa with a big tray filled with tiny red glasses of Grandma's red currant wine. Each child could have one teaspoonful carefully poured from the glass-stopped decanter. This ritual inspired my friend, Rich Jardine, to write a little ditty which he sang to the tune of "A Hot Time in the Old Town" at one of our parties.

> Joe and Tom and Tommy Goodey
> They think they are so fine.
> They all go down to Barsons
> And they have a little wine.
> But the best of all to tell it
> Is to see Phil and Bessie shine.
> There'll be a hot time at Barsons tonight.

After our little sip, we sang "Blue Bell," "Cheyenne," and "Shine On, Harvest Moon." Then would come the climax. Grandpa would call out, "All Democrats please stand." Several sleepy adherents of the said party would arise. I was torn between conflicting emotions. I wanted to please Grandpa, but there sat my dad, the lone Republican in the crowd. I usually compromised by hiding behind some grown-up and maintaining my neutrality.

The old sofa was spread out for a family bed and kids cuddled down in every direction. A fortunate few who didn't fit were carried off to Grandma's bed where they could sink in the feathers with that pleasant feeling of going down, down, down.

The adults quickly began a game of High Five.

"Look at the spades I had to throw away."

"If you had just made hearts trump, see how I could have helped you."

"What did you have in clubs or diamonds?" Now and then I peeked out to see who were the winners, but I soon fell asleep.

About twelve o'clock, our laughing parents roused us again and snuggled us down in the sleigh to go home. As

I cuddled in the straw and munched sleepily on another doughnut, I thought how lucky I was to have a grandpa with a farm and a big house—above all, how lucky I was to have a grandpa who liked fun.

The old farmhouse is bare now and falling to decay. Spiders swing gaily from their tangled webs on the sagging porches. Trash and feathers poke out of the fancy gables which have become a haven for sparrows. Tall bunch grass has choked out the long native currant row, and weeds lift their seedy heads over Grandma's pansy bed. The silver maples are brown and dead, but the initials P. B. and M. B., for Grandpa Peter and Grandma Mary Ellen Barson still glare from the dried bark. A tall pine stands in front of the graveled driveway like a stiff soldier guarding the memories of the past. But if that old house could speak, what tales of joy and family devotion it could tell!

*Note:* This story won a prize in the Cache Valley Centennial writing contest of 1956.

## *Past Winters*

Here are some newspaper clippings, yellowed with age, that I found pasted in an old book belonging to my Grandfather Barson, written for the *Logan Journal* under the name of "Sanko":

### 23 February 1897

We have a brand new clock and a new floor in our meeting house, and when we get our new chandeliers the hall will show up well.

Last Wednesday evening our chapel was lit up and the people were seated, with plenty of picnic on hand, waiting for the arrival of Caroline Thompson, to give her a genuine surprise. At 8 o'clock she arrived. When she was seated the choir sang "Love at Home." After the opening prayer everyone sang "Auld Lang Zyne." Then came a speech by John Buttars, followed by the Highland Fling by Katie and Laura Griffiths and a speech by Andrew Heggie. Then there was a step dance by Bishop Jardine and his wife. This was followed by a step dance by six young men, P.S. Barson, John Buttars, Frank Griffin, James G. Thompson, Walter Thompson and Jack Thompson.

Caroline Thompson then spoke, after which she was presented with a handsome rocking chair. With tears in her eyes she thanked the people for it.

The program was continued until ten o'clock, when all present sat down and partook of a chicken dinner; there was also sorghum, squash pie, oranges, and candy. Then the benches were removed and you ought to have seen us dance. At 12 o'clock the curtain dropped and thus ended a beautiful day.

### December 1927

For a number of years it seemed that it was impossible to raise grain in this section, many crops being a total failure. At the present time, conditions have changed and fall grain is the chief agricultural crop.

We are pleased with a number of beautiful natural springs west of town which feed our present water system. The springs north of town are used for irrigation purposes and help in the production of an abundant alfalfa crop.

Conditions have materially changed here in fifty years. At the early date the people met in a log cabin, 28 by 17 feet, and the hut was used for a school house. The population has continued to increase until we now boast 640 citizens. The farmers' slogan here is to keep out of debt and they are working hard toward that end.

### 1928

With the number of new pianos and radio sets just

sold and others ordered by Santa, Clarkston should never want for sweet music on the air. Nearly every home has some kind of musical instrument to aid our younger generation to obtain a musical education and refine their characters and at the same time join recreation with pleasure.

### January 28, 1929

Our Clarkston correspondent phoned over this morning to let us know of weather conditions there. Even before last night's storm, snow was so deep that milk wagons couldn't run and in order that the milk might not be wasted the farmers are churning the cream into butter. The school bus conveying students to North Cache High School was also unable to run, and the mail was carried out by horseback as in days of yore. This is the deepest snow our town has experienced in forty years.

And now to repeat the words of my Grandfather, "The curtain comes down. It has been a beautiful day."

## *These I Remember*

I'd like to hear again the song of the teakettle as it bubbled on a coal range. I'd like to watch the lid of that teakettle bob up and down by the light of a coal oil lamp and feel the message of peace that it gave me. The frost working its way through on the door hinges and the white designs growing thicker and thicker on the window panes held no terror as the teakettle sang. There was peace without and peace within, the "peace that passeth understanding."

I'd like to hear the sound of the fiddle as my dad sawed squeaky tones on its strings, and the mellow notes of my mother's alto voice as she sang, "The Lord Is My Shepherd."

I'd like to hear the patter of rain on the shingles as I slept in a loft. We were three to a bed, but no one thought we were crowded.

I'd like to hear the croaking of frogs in the meadow on a still summer night, the sound of the anvil as the blacksmith pounded out horseshoes, the sleigh bells on a frosty night as the horses climbed over drifts of snow.

I'd like to smell grease rendering in the oven and big kettles full of melting fat on the stove. I'd like to smell cracklings made into soap, the pungent smell of lye, the spearmint along the ditch bank by the foot bridge, the pink meadow flowers on their long, straight stems and the marshy dampness of the meadow, where I walked with the cows

I remember the scent of Johnny-jump-ups struggling for survival in the weeds along the sidewalk, a glass full of "roosters" (dog-toothed violets) fresh from Long Hill, and the bark from the willow as my dad made me a whistle.

Mustard pickles and chili sauce sent their aroma outside as I came home from school.

How could I forget the scent of the slimy looking mushrooms that Dad brought from the ranch and the heavy smell (that reminded me of chloroform) rising from stacks of wheat in the field with tall sunflowers growing all around them? Nor could I forget the scent of the little bag of asafetida I wore around my neck to ward off colds.

I'd like to feel the print of my body on a bed tick filled with fresh straw. If no one shook the straw, my anatomy would fit into the same mold each night with exact precision.

I'd like to feel the thick woolen stockings that my grandmother knit for me, which both burned and tickled my feet. If they were not washed frequently, I had to wear them on the same foot each day, otherwise the point where my big toe had been made a lump over the little toe on the opposite foot. These stockings could become so stiff with sweat that they looked as if they had been molded into shape with plaster. I'd like to feel my shoes laced tight around my ankles, with my long-handled underwear tucked neatly into them to cover the ridge, and yes, I'd even like to experience again the discomfort of a bath in a tin tub.

I'd like to feel the thrill of Christmas morning, when Christmas was reserved only for December and when toys were truly appreciated. I'd like to know again the joy of a buggy ride with plenty of moonlight.

I'd like to taste home-ground sausage flavored with sage from the garden, buttermilk poured fresh from the churn, the mustard and dandelion greens my grandmother said would purify our blood in the spring, the dried apples that hung on strings tied up in the attic, the rock candy that was a delicacy for Christmas, the honey in the comb straight from the hive, or "head cheese" which was the meat boiled from a hog's head, chopped, seasoned and pressed in a cloth bag.

How could I forget the monotonous winter diet of salt pork, potatoes, beans, and dried apples?

I'd like to see once again a man with a team mowing or raking hay, six horses pushing a grain harvester, and the men with header boxes unloading the grain, that header crew in the old ranch house at the dinner table with their good-natured banter, the steam thresher with its big iron wheels, the water boy, an old-fashioned derrick, the boy on the cart that pulled the big Jackson fork of hay up on the stack, and the call of "Trip!" to release it.

I want to see a wedding with really practical gifts—tin tubs, water buckets, dish pans, brooms, pots and pans, wash boards, combs and scissors.

The little town of Clarkston can no longer be called "Isolated", because it is now connected with all the modern conveniences of the times. We can look back at our oddities without apology knowing we had the basic qualities of love, cooperation, and honesty, some missing in today's modern world. How proud our ancestors must have been to see log houses replace the old fort, and then a rock meetinghouse erected, and beside it a school. There we were taught the 3 R's, all that was deemed necessary for a successful life. Then our people saw the prophesy of Brigham Young fulfilled that the sage brush hills would some day wave with golden grain. Green trees and flower gardens now adorn modern homes, and "Old Gunsight" stands majestically in the background guarding the peace and tranquility of the past.

I drive up the street, where I used to live, and say with the poet, "How dear to my heart are the scenes of my childhood." Memories engulf me, so I stop by the side of the road, and enjoy a dip into the past. I am a child again playing with rag dolls, and trimming cabbage leaf hats with chicken feathers, and little yellow Johnny-jump-ups that grew along the sidewalk. I ride my sled down this same road, and see the big snow banks. I see little kids blowing willow whistles, and spinning tops made from spools. I see boys on wooden stilts, or some made with cans and tied with binder twine. The corner is still there where we toasted potatoes in the dry leaves in the fall, and there is the yard where we played "Hide and Seek" and "Run Sheep Run," in the evenings. We had ball games in that same yard. The balls were made from worn out woolen stockings and covered with soft leather from old shoes—the work of some patient mother.

Thanks to memories, my heart is overflowing.

Clarkston is now on the map too. Every year a pageant honoring Martin Harris is presented in the amphitheater. This pageant attracts the general authorities of the church as well as people from far and near. We felt in a class all by ourselves to have Martin Harris buried in our cemetery, the man who saw the angel and the gold plates, and never denied that testimony. That was our legacy.

I look back with joy and appreciation to my family, friends, and teachers for a happy childhood in spite of primitive conditions, and I can say, as we sing, I love those dear hearts and gentle people that live in my hometown.

All these people, all these things I will remember. . . always.

*A Very, Very Lovely Book of Memories.*

*Eva Riley Adams.*